BLESSED HOPE

SARAH GRIFFITH LUND
& CHAD ABBOTT

BLESSED HOPE

90 DAILY DEVOTIONS FOR MENTAL HEALTH AND FAITH

chalice
PRESS

Cover Design: Mila Graphic Design
Interior Design: Connie H.C. Wang

Print: 9780827203594
EPUB: 9780827203600
EPDF: 9780827203617

ChalicePress.com

Printed in the United States of America

Dedicated to Carter with all my heart. You are my sunshine.
—SGL

For Lukki and Isa, because your wholeness means everything to me.
—CA

Dear Readers,

We write as pastors from the perspectives of our personal lived experiences at the intersection of mental health and faith. *Blessed Hope* is a spiritual resource designed to accompany a holistic approach to mental well-being. We encourage readers to explore spiritual practices and also seek various mental health supports from professional counseling and therapeutic services, medical care, including medications, and peer support groups. There is no shame in needing help. Mental health is physical health and everyone deserves mental health care.

You deserve care, support, and love. Our deepest hope is to encourage your spirit, especially on the hard days, reminding you of your worth and value. May the words and stories of blessed hope in these pages offer you an inner resource of courage for the living of these days. God loves you.

With hope for today,
Pastor Sarah and Pastor Chad

Contents

Introduction

"Hope is the thing with feathers."
—Emily Dickinson

What can we do in the face of increasing depression and anxiety? We purposefully cultivate hope. That's what this book invites us to do. One day at a time, one person at a time, in community with others. We boldly proclaim with the saints and prophets of old that nothing, including depression and anxiety, can separate us from God's love. The opposite of hope is despair, and despair is a form of soul death. Neither depression, nor anxiety, nor any kind of mental health experience can deny our God-given right to hope. This book is an invitation for you to join the spiritual movement to cultivate hope as a spiritual practice.

Prayer itself, in all its manifestations, is an act of hope. Prayer is a bold act of deep resistance to the traumatic forces and shadows that surround us. When we pray, we dare to call upon God to engage us and move us from a fragmented world toward a world made whole. Prayer takes courage, especially when depression and anxiety tell us we don't deserve God's love. Prayer can feel lonely. This book reminds you that you are not alone. The Spirit unites us as one human family through prayer, devotion, and meditation, providing spiritual grounding to embody what poet James Crews calls "the sacrament of hope."[1]

This book offers you the gift of a community where we bear witness to one another's diverse mental health experiences and boldly proclaim: just as you are, right now in this moment, you are loved. We offer a word of hope to bless you each day. We remind you that no matter who you are or what you are going through, God created you in the image of divine love, and you are a blessing to this world. Each devotional entry is designed to connect you to God's story in scripture, our stories as companions along the way, and your unfolding story as a person designed by God to carry a song of hope in your soul. The trouble is when we forget our song, grow too weary to sing, or become overwhelmed by the pain of life and detach from our song of heart. Losing hope is a form of soul death, and the experience can be crushing. This book provides words of comfort and encouragement because this is what we needed in times of despair in our own lives.

What is Hope?

Hope is more than a daydream. Hope is putting one foot in front of the other, or rolling forward, especially when we feel trapped and stuck because of overwhelming fear. As daily experiences of anxiety and

[1] James Crews, "Writing for Refuge," webinar, March 2026.

depression become commonplace, hope feels far away for many people. Despair, numbness, and exhaustion disrupt our sense of connection to God. Our souls drown in weariness. We wonder: "Where is God? Has God forgotten about me and abandoned me?" We ask for God to have mercy and to give us some relief for our mental anguish; our psychaches. Psychache is a term coined by suicidologist Edwin Shneidman to describe unbearable psychological pain — an all-consuming internal anguish that eclipses every other experience. We long to be comforted, for our emotional wounds to be healed. We long to be loved and accepted for who we are, no matter the status of our mental health.

This is why claiming our birthright to hope during the wide spectrum of mental health experiences is critical work of the soul. Poet Emily Dickinson famously wrote, "Hope is the thing with feathers / That perches in the soul, / And sings the tune without the words, / And never stops at all."[2] If hope is something with feathers perching on our soul that never stops, then hope is active, vibrant, and stubborn. Hope keeps us alive. Hope can get us through the day and the long night. Hope courageously enters the messiness of life, places of despair, and dares to light a candle toward a new day.

Mental Health and Hope

As people intimately connected to the shadow side of depression and anxiety because of our own past and current lived experiences with mental health, we seek God's comfort anew each day. Spiritual practices like prayer are what can help keep us grounded in hope. Persistent prayer is a spiritual practice that may help keep hope alive. For many of us, depression obliterates hope, and no amount of prayer awakens it for us. There is no shame in losing touch with hope. All of us, at some point in our lives, will experience the loss of hope. This is where being connected to community can help because community, at its best, surrounds us with hope. Imagine being in the presence of a songbird alive with hope. Even though in times of despair, we may not be able to sing our own song of hope, we are not abandoned and left alone in silence. Faith communities sing the song of hope with us and for us. We testify to the power of belonging to faith communities throughout the course of one's life, through the valleys of depression and on the mountaintops of joy, and everywhere in between. Pastor Sarah's childhood church, Broadway Christian Church (Disciples of Christ) in Columbia, Missouri, was a deep source of hope for her during times of despair caused by chronic and serious mental health episodes in her family. Hope was nurtured by the community of people gathering each week around the communion table

[2] Emily Dickinson, *The Poems of Emily Dickinson,* ed. R.W. Franklin (Harvard University Press, 1999).

of God's love. Hope was knowing there was a place for her at the table. Hope didn't make problems go away, but hope made the problems not the only story to tell. Hope was showing up, eating the bread, drinking the juice, singing the songs, and saying the prayers.

If hope were only heroic, large-scale, or dramatic leaps of the soul, then what would happen when the soul gets tired and weary? Faith communities are songbirds of hope. The songbird of hope is persistent. She shows us the transformational power of daily, small, and intentional acts of resistance in a world bent on the destruction of our peace.

Like the songbird, hope desires to take flight within us, lifting us out of despair. Yes, sometimes hopelessness can cause the songbird to hesitate to flap her wings and take flight. What happens when the songbird of hope feels like she cannot take flight because of the weight of despair? We know this heavy feeling of carrying the weight of despair and not being able to lift ourselves up out of despair by our own strength. This is where we are reminded of our need for community. Our inner light of hope is one small flickering flame that joins with another and then another when we connect in communities of hope. Spaces that were once dim transform into sanctuaries of light, creating incubators of hope. The sacred story of Jesus' mother, Mary, illustrates how hope can grow in shadows, as Mary gave birth to the holy child, the Light of the world.

Whether today is a good day or a tough day for your mental health, daily spiritual practices can help keep us grounded in hope. Nurturing our inner light of hope is an act of faith that supports positive mental health. As people of faith, we can use daily prayer practices as radical acts in resistance of reclaiming our God-given hope. In a world that worships false idols of peace and happiness (materialism, power, popularity, and wealth, just to name a few), true and lasting peace and joy come from daily tending to the flame of our inward spirit. Hope is what sparks our inner light.

Poet and writer Nikita Gill knows this spiritual practice of hope well. She says, "My grandmother used to say 'hope is a doing thing, not just a feeling thing.' Which is to say that hope is an action, not only an emotion. Which is to say that to be hopeful is not just to dream, but to use your hands to build a better world."[3] A better world is built by hands open to hope and hands reaching for hope. We hope because we acknowledge the current state of things is temporary and dare to believe that a new world is coming.

It is easy to feel discouraged by abuses of power, cruelty, broken relationships and broken hearts, violence upon violence, and the shadows of oppressive forces in the world that press upon our hearts and bodyminds. If that were the only story we told ourselves, then it

---

[3] Nikita Gill (@nikita_gill), Instagram, November 25, 2025, https://www.instagram.com/p/DRfExZPCE5k/.

would be hard to imagine the feathers of Dickinson or join the building hands of Gill's grandmother. Hope tells a different story, one that is born in a million different ways across the landscapes of human lives, in part because each of us is born in the likeness and image of a God who is expansive and vast in expression.

In fact, we sense that while some may claim we are wired for connection, others demonstrate through science that we are wired for the spiritual. As people born of community and of the Spirit, we are wired to seek hope in its varied expressions. This is the work of the Spirit. One way to tend to the inward flame of the Spirit to cultivate hope is to spend time in meditation, reflection, and prayer.

Faith and Hope

Faith in God helps us trust that hope is eschatological, a vision of an already, but not yet, reality. God has already overcome all things with the love made known to us in Christ, and yet the world is being made whole and restored into the likeness of a God known to us as Love. This means we use our hands to build a new world, to co-create a loving, compassionate world with God. We put ourselves out into the world one act of kindness, justice, and hope at a time, even when it is scary to do so. We tell the true stories about our lives, and this is how we heal. We create art, sing songs, grab groceries for a neighbor, go to therapy, spend time in nature, write a poem, rest and sleep, and accompany others in their grief because we know that each of these small ways of living allows us to move closer toward a world reborn.

As we welcome you to this devotional book of hope, we welcome you as friends. We invite you to enter this space knowing we each hold with open hands a part of us and the world that is hurting and in need of healing. We understand healing to be of a spiritual nature, a repairing of our sense of belovedness, being loved completely and totally just as we are, no exceptions, by a God who created us in love. Being whole is not about being perfect. Being whole is about staying connected to the divine source of love.

We are unashamed to name how our mental health is interconnected with our spiritual health. We desire to shine a light of hope in the shadows of mental health experiences that can feel overwhelming, isolating, and despairing. No mental health stories are identical. We all have important differences that make our personal experiences with mental health unique. What we do share is the common human desire to love and to be loved, no matter our mental health status. This book reminds you that you are worthy of God's love. This is our greatest hope.

We come to prayer and devotional life looking for a word that can call us toward hope. These devotionals of hope are our way of taking the fragmented pieces and mending them through the power of story, vulnerability, prayers, and loving ourselves and the world until we are reconnected to the tapestry of God's love. In these pages, we seek to expand your imagination for what hope can look like in the world. Through each story, each sacred word, each opened door into our vulnerable journeys, you are invited to uncover what you are holding close that needs healing. We invite you to reflect on your own stories of mental health. Invite God's light of love to shine upon the places most tender to you. There is no shame in being human. To tell the true stories of our lives is to heal.

Hope is healing. Hope is a key ingredient for our spiritual and mental health. It is our prayer not only that you will find the hope that lives within your journey, but also that you will encounter a community of others who care deeply about a life of faith and the power of tending to our mental health journey with deep and abiding care. In fact, we would go so far as to suggest that stories and words of hope such as these are not only life-giving but lifesaving and suicide prevention. We encourage you to consider inviting others to read this book with you and to spend time in conversation and prayer. Hope is contagious, and sharing this book of hope with others is one way to strengthen your own reservoir of hope.

Lifesaving work is grounded in a theology that suggests our hope is not just our own but born out of carrying one another in community. Some days you may not feel as though you have the flame of hope within you. That is okay. You are not alone. The strength of faith communities tending to the work of mental health is that we don't have to have it all together or have it all figured out to experience hope. Though there are days when we do not carry hope, others can do the holy work of building sacred spaces for us to be ourselves, and we can draw upon their hope. Hope is communal work. We need each other. We hold hope for one another.

The good news is ultimately that our hope is in God, particularly a God who reminds us through the power of the Resurrection that death, oppression, depression, and destruction do not have the last word. This God is making all things new, inviting us to dare to believe that things in this world can change and that we ourselves can change. Such hope is what sustains us. This is the hope we are invited to experience and share with a hurting world.

Friendship and Hope

Our friendship as colleagues has been one of the candle flames of hope in our lives. Our professional as well as our spiritual journeys have had the great privilege of intersecting at different points. We first met in a seminary classroom where we stood in solidarity with our Queer seminary siblings and began to discern the futures God intended for our ministries. Over the years, our families have shared meals together and welcomed the

Spirit's holy nudges. We have also sat with one another through the harder moments in life, like health scares, and in these times of uncertainty we offered one another affirmation and encouragement through prayer. We have supported one another's parenting and vocational journeys. Our shared passion for tending to the spiritual life and for caring for mental health binds us together.

Out of friendship and shared ministry, a vision for the threading together of these passions came to light in this book. We wondered about the words we receive in the new year, Epiphany season, known as "star words" as the guiding lights into this devotional. Over the years, we both received a word for the year that guides us, challenges us, grounds us, or inspires us. Because this practice has been so meaningful to the intersection of our spiritual lives with our mental health, we started to see these words as potential daily words of inspiration and guidance specifically to encourage you, no matter where you are on your spiritual and mental health journey.

How to Find Hope with This Book

Epiphany is a season to celebrate the presence of Christ in the world and in our lives. In some traditions, for Epiphany people select or are given a special word to focus on for the year. For example, one year Sarah's star word was "curiosity." One year Chad's word was "bless." The hope is for these star words to remind us of the light of Christ's presence in our daily journey. These "blessed words" can invoke the presence of God in our daily lives, a "blessed hope" grounding us for spiritual living as we care for our collective mental health. These devotions are designed to be a year-round resource.

We start each daily devotion with a word to shine a light of hope on your path. We prayed about which words to use for the devotional, and we followed the lead of the Holy Spirit in selecting each word for each day. We trust that the Spirit blesses you with the word you need, when you need it. In each daily devotion we provide a scripture verse, a meditation, a suggested reflection activity to guide your exploration of the topic, and a prayer for the day.

In this devotional, we invite you into these ninety days with sacred words that can inspire your faith and support positive mental health. We invite you to join us in embracing hope that is filled with action and transformation. All devotions are authored by either Pastor Sarah or Pastor Chad, except the last devotion on hope, which we wanted to write together. Some devotions explicitly recommend resources or ways of seeking better mental health; some share illustrations of personal experiences of mental health; some speak of ways spirituality benefits mental health; and some are intended to encourage more compassionate ways of living. We use language reflecting the fluidity and spectrum of mental health and we try to avoid language that stigmatizes mental health. Feel free to engage with this book in whatever way blesses you, whether that's reading it through from beginning to end or hopping around. We invite you to read this book alone as a private time with God or together in a group or with a prayer partner.

If hope were simply about wishful thinking and dreaming, this would be a very different book. We testify to the messiness of living a life of hope. This is a book of invitation into a faith that is healing and lifesaving because it is spiritually active and pregnant with authentic hope. As you bathe your soul with these blessed words, may they provide hope for your faith and your mental health. We are witnesses to the interconnectedness of hope. We sing the song of hope with you, for you, alongside you, and around you. Together, hope is our blessed song.

With abundant hope,
Pastor Sarah and Pastor Chad

Beginning

In the beginning, when God created the heavens and the earth...
—Genesis 1:1

I'll never forget my father-in-law, Joe, standing at the hearth of his new home, hand on the mantle and tears in his eyes. Over the years, my wife's parents lived in apartments, townhouses, or church parsonages but never owned their own home. In 2008, they bought their first home, and this threshold moment was filled with hope for the years of family, laughter, grief, joy, and animal companions, and all that was to come. This brief pause at their hearth offered a sacred acknowledgment of the important role beginnings play in reaching toward hope.

While beginnings are hopeful, there are dueling energies present when we begin something new. Beginnings can be simultaneously exciting and scary. When the excitement is present, the possibility of hope for our relationships, vocations, institutions, communities, marriages, families, education, and businesses radiates. When it is scary, it is because beginnings also carry significant uncertainty or lack clarity about an unknown future.

Most of us see beginnings as anticipatory, as moments for creation of the new. Yet I have also found myself focusing on all the failure that is possible or all the anxiety of the unknown. We can hold both the anxiety and the excitement of beginnings with tenderness and compassion for ourselves. We might even look to the opening words of the Hebrew testament story of creation: "In the beginning when God created the heavens and the earth." This famous story of origins tells us right from the start that beginnings are about creating the new, and such an understanding of beginning grounds us in the idea that God is generative in relationship to us and the earth.

We are accompanied through all the hopeful possibilities and the anxiety of what the future holds. No matter what we face, God is present at whatever hearth awaits us in our new beginnings. Beginnings offer us a threshold moment at the hearth of our own hearts, an opening into mental health and well-being daily. As you cross over new thresholds in your life, what possibilities await you?

Reflection Activity: What might you create that can bring life and new beginnings into the world? Consider creating a hearth or sacred altar space where you can ritualize your threshold moments.

Prayer: When hope seems dim, O God, help me to begin again. Amen.

With hope for today,
Pastor Chad

Courage

"Take heart, it is I; do not be afraid."—Mark 6:50

Our mental health is impacted by past events, current situations, the environment, biology, and societal factors. Natural disasters such as hurricanes, floods, fires, and tornadoes often cause people to experience post-traumatic stress disorder because of the acute and long-term impact of stress, uncertainty, loss, and chaos. In the story of Jesus calming the waters in the gospel, the disciples were stressed because their lives flashed before them during the storm. They were preparing for their boat to capsize. Then they were frightened by Jesus' appearance walking on water. Jesus offered them words of comfort as he came to be with them in the midst of the storm. When we are afraid, we can pray for the presence of Jesus to help calm our inner storms.

In the face of my own fears, I pray for courage. The Latin root of the word courage is *cor*, which means "heart." When I engage in public speaking about mental health and faith, including sharing some of my personal stories about experiences with the stigma and shame our society places on mental health and disabilities, I always feel a little scared. I notice my mind immediately races to avoid self-exposure. I wonder, *What if instead of sharing my story, I share the startling statistics about suicide rates, depression, and anxiety?* While data are foundational for research and advocacy, when it comes to ending the stigma and shame, there's nothing like the power of stories to break the silence and dismantle stigma.

Being authentic and vulnerable when it comes to mental health can feel scary. Like the disciples, it can feel like we are in the midst of a storm, not sure when it will end and what the damage will be when it's over. It takes courage for me every time I choose to share my mental health experiences because I am bumping up against centuries of church teachings that cast shame and blame on lack of faith, sinfulness, demon possession, immorality, and laziness as the primary causes of disability and mental health experiences. Leading from the heart takes courage. It's okay to feel scared when you are doing something hard. It takes courage to say no to people, places, activities, and things that no longer bless you. The ability to say no improves my mental health and gives me hope.

Be comforted knowing you are not alone. God sends a comforter, the Holy Spirit, to be with you in your heart. Remember, the drumbeat of courage comes from deep within your heart. Every time you honor your true stories, it is an act of courage. Jesus reminds us that truth has the power to calm the storms.

Reflection Activity: Place a hand over your heart or be still and draw your attention to the physical beating rhythm of your heartbeat. Repeat this affirmation three times: "In my heart there is courage."

Prayer: God of hope, grant me enough courage for today. Amen.

With hope for today,
Pastor Sarah

Invitation

"Listen! I am standing at the door, knocking; if you hear my voice and open the door, I will come to you and eat with you, and you with me."
—Revelation 3:20

One morning, sitting on the front porch of a retreat center with my tea while listening to the birds sing, praying, tending to my mental health, and journaling, I heard voices in the distance. Emerging from the forest were three pilgrims walking in the woods. They asked if I would like to join them, so I put on my hiking boots and accepted their invitation. As part of the journey, we walked through a piece of land known as the "Paths of Mindfulness," a patch of tall grass with paths mowed for walking and praying. One pilgrim said that with all the distractions of the world and the daily pain we experience, we need a space for our minds to heal. He said these paths were an invitation into letting go. Right there, among the grass-mown paths, I let go of my pain, trauma, and worry. And a door opened into a deep encounter with God, allowing my mind to heal.

Reflecting on this experience, I sense that each day, each moment, each breath is an invitation into encounter and connection with the holy. In spiritual direction, a frequent question is, "What might be the invitation here?" or "What might God be inviting you into?" Revelation 3:20 suggests that God comes directly to us, knocking on our door, inviting us to dine together. Imagine that! We are invited to dine with God! How is God's invitation present in a situation that is difficult, in a relationship at work that needs tending, as we care for our own mental health, or in discerning a vocational change? Whether we are invited to dine with God or to a walk in the woods, healing our hearts and minds is possible.

Reflection Activity: How might you better notice invitations from God in daily living? Grab a small notebook or use a note-taking app on your phone for when those daily invitations appear so you can take notes and respond.

Prayer: When hope seems dim, O God, and you knock at the door, help me to be open to the invitation on the other side. Amen.

With hope for today,
Pastor Chad

Question

Then Jesus said to them, "I ask you, is it lawful to do good or to do harm on the sabbath, to save life or to destroy it?"—Luke 6:9

In the healing stories of the Bible, like this one about the man with a hand disability, Jesus demonstrates his healing power by taking away the person's disability. But it's hard to understand what this healing story means for us today. Does Jesus take away physical disabilities today? Does Jesus take away mental health experiences that are painful? Healing a person with a disability was the action that got Jesus in trouble. The purpose of the story is to demonstrate Jesus breaking the rule about not working on the Sabbath. But it raises important questions for us about the way disability and healing are talked about in the Bible.

It is good to question the ways stories like this one historically (and still today) are often used by people in the church to portray people with disabilities as somehow spiritually inferior and broken, in need of saving or healing. There is power in questioning this interpretation and offering alternative ways to understand the meaning of the story today. The story ends with the religious teachers and Pharisees in the synagogue enraged by Jesus' disobedience because he healed on the Sabbath. Jesus questioned the rules and then broke them. This upset the status quo.

What if the man with the hand disability also had a non-apparent disability, like major depression? What does it mean that Jesus desires for us to experience healing no matter what barriers society creates? Could we think about the synagogue authorities as gatekeepers to affordable and accessible health care? How might that change the way we interpret the story?

We are empowered to question the biblical text. God can handle our questions. We can grow closer to God through the searching for truth, especially as we seek to reclaim stories that once were used to cause harm. Disabilities and mental health experiences are not punishments from God, nor given to us by God to make us stronger. What kind of God would give a child panic attacks? This is not the work of God; instead, panic attacks are caused by other realities, often human-made, such as environment, circumstances, biology, or society. What God does give us is unconditional love to help ground us and regulate us in the midst of life's ups and downs.

Centering the well-being of people with disabilities and people with mental health experiences is important to the sustaining of hope. I once heard a neuroscientist say that we wouldn't think of asking a person wearing glasses to throw their glasses in the trash and just pray for better vision. During my first visit with my eye doctor, I was amazed at how much better I could see with prescription lenses. I question people who spiritualize disabilities and mental health realities. Sometimes we need glasses and antidepressants to improve our quality of life. God uses medicine and science to help us.

In the act of questioning things that don't ring true to our experiences and questioning the status quo, we claim our power and agency. This is an act of courageous hope. We ask the hard questions, trusting in the goodness and love of God.

Reflection Activity: What question burning inside of you have you been too afraid to ask? Close your eyes and place your palms facing up or relaxed and open to God's presence. Invite God to place a question in your hands or in your heart. May today be about living this question.

Prayer: God of hope, bless me with questions to awaken my soul. Amen.

With hope for today,
Pastor Sarah

Rest

"Come away to a deserted place all by yourselves and rest a while."
—Mark 6:31

Rest is essential to our humanity and thriving as God's beloved children. We live in a culture commanding our every waking moment to be productive, a deception built upon the idea that unrelenting work, over-functioning, and achieving more are what make a successful life. We need more balance; we need more rest. Rest is an act of defiant hope. It defies what production demands. The times I have struggled the most with anxiety and depression have been the times I neglected to pause for rest; and when I chose rest, I felt lighter and more resilient.

I have one of the best coworkers. One day, she and I were talking on the phone about a project. I was finding myself overwhelmed by all the things I needed to do, and in the midst of it all, I was supposed to be taking some much-needed time away. I suggested that I find ways of squeezing in all the work despite my exhaustion. My coworker replied, "Or maybe you just don't worry about that until you are back from your time away? All will be well. We can handle everything else while you are away." She gave me permission to take the actual rest my bodymind and spirit so desperately needed.

We don't give one another permission in our culture to rest. What might it be like to build rest into how we live in community with each other or into our work environments? Certainly, Jesus implored his disciples to get away and rest for a while. Not just on occasion after they had achieved all the markers of success—no, right in the middle of all the demands of the crowds around them, Jesus knew that rest demanded to be part of the rhythm and flow of their lives.

How can we take Jesus' approach to work and rest and live into the rest that is our birthright? How can we be intentional about more pauses in our life? God invites us to rest in hope.

Reflection Activity: Take a nap. Pause what you are doing, and breathe. Take a full day away from unnecessary screens and technology, and pay attention to how different your body feels when you rest. Choose to do something that is rejuvenating.

Prayer: When hope seems dim, O God, let me rest in you. Amen.

With hope for today,
Pastor Chad

Dare

Dare to speak the word with greater boldness and without fear.
—Philippians 1:14

A dare is a Spirit nudge. We dare to hope. We dare to dream. We dare to break free of toxic elements of our culture. We dare to tell a bolder story about our own belovedness. We dare to live in the authenticity of who God created us to be. Recently, my clergy leadership coach reminded me of the power of trusting the Spirit's movement in my life, even if it is just barely noticeable. Micro-nudge; the smallest hint of shifting energy. I wonder what it would look like to be unafraid to hope. Why might we fear hope?

Hope fuels change. To keep the status quo, society is filled with distractions from hope. We move at such a fast pace through our "to-do" lists. We are rewarded with dopamine for being distracted by our devices. Juggling multiple tasks at one time is the norm. To break free from the grind culture of productivity and perfectionism is to dare to embrace what it means to be fully human. We are not machines. We are not robots. We are flesh. We are imperfect. We are human.

I took a mental health day once on a Sunday. *On Sunday.* I am a local church preacher, and preachers are supposed to be in the pulpit every Sunday. However, the night before had been emotionally rough, and I was on the phone with a dear friend late into the night. She prayed with me and brought me comfort, reminding me that the awful feeling would not last forever. I let my church leaders know I was taking a sick day. My brain needed rest. My soul needed rest.

I am grateful I dared to ask for what I needed and the church provided the support to make that mental health day possible. A retired minister filled the pulpit for me with less than twelve hours' notice. Bless them. It's no accident this same retired minister was the one who led my church to becoming a WISE church for mental health (Welcoming, Inclusive, Supportive, and Engaged).

Dare to be enfleshed. Dare to stop over-functioning. Dare to take a mental health day. We can improve our mental health when we honor work-life boundaries, taking sick days, mental health days, and vacation days whenever possible.

Reflection Activity: Dare yourself to notice the Spirit nudging you today as you set aside the urgency of now. Trust the Spirit to carry you through this day.

Prayer: God of hope, reveal the truth and let me dare to be my true self. Amen.

With hope for today,
Pastor Sarah

Blessing

God bless you and keep you; God make God's face to shine upon you and be gracious to you; God lift up God's countenance upon you and give you peace.
—Numbers 6:24–26

I spent a short time in my twenties as a community organizer on the near east side of Indianapolis, serving dozens of neighborhoods as they sought to flourish in a part of town with high rates of poverty. The organization I served worked with churches to help change the landscape of the city as it faced rising crime, prostitution, drugs, and increased violence. In my first week in the role, I asked a clergy colleague, who had spent two decades serving in the community, how I might best serve the neighborhoods. His response was, "Chad, speak words of blessing. The biblical word for 'blessing' translates as 'to speak well of.' You need to speak well of the residents and the place where they live. They have spent nearly four decades being told just how terrible a place it is where they live. Tell them something different. Remind them that they are sacred and that where they live matters. Remind them that hope is not lost. Speak words of blessing."

We live in a world where it is so easy to start from the negative, from a perspective of lack or scarcity. We can easily speak of what neighborhoods or people lack or how they do not measure up to some impossible standard. This can easily create negative self-talk within ourselves or our communities that do not adequately reflect our being made in the divine image.

What would our world be like if we were to speak words of blessing first to ourselves and to our neighbors? Would we have the kind of peace the Bible refers to? I am not dismissing the struggles or pain of our broken systems, nor am I implying a pollyanna faith that cozies up to a prosperity version of God's relationship to us. Instead of beginning with deficiencies and failures, we might move more toward healing these misguided stories we tell ourselves and our communities if we could begin with the assumption that every person we come across is worthy of blessing. This could bring hope to circumstances that have longed for hope for a long time. How might our mental health be different with this view of the world that is abundantly blessed?

Reflection Activity: Today I invite you to share words of blessing with your family members, coworkers, the driver who cut you off, or that neighbor going through a hard time. It just might change everything.

Prayer: When hope seems dim, O God, blessing others just might transform the world. May it be so. Amen.

With hope for today,
Pastor Chad

Truth

I have no greater joy than this, to know that my children are walking in the truth.—3 John 1:4

The truth is that today I had a hard time getting going. I wanted to stay in my pajamas and bathrobe. I wanted another cup of coffee. I wanted to sit on my couch and stare out the window. I wanted to do nothing. I wanted to rest.

Instead, I pushed through the inertia that begs me to stop. The truth is I am afraid of what might happen if I stop. What would I notice in my bodymind? What feelings might bubble up inside of me? What thoughts would creep into my mind?

What truth is my bodymind communicating? What is the cost of ignoring my bodymind's truth?

Staying busy with work and distractions are numbing techniques hiding the truth of my well-being. If I am honest, I need to take a mental health day. But I'm too busy to stop being busy! (Yeah, that doesn't make sense. I am trying to be gentle with myself.)

During my sabbatical, I explored connecting to joy in nature, joy in my bodymind, and joy in my relationships with friends. I discovered the truth that when I slow down long enough, I discover joy all around me. Joy is among the birds that sing, in the way my bodymind stretches toward the sun, in the gentle smile of a friend over a cup of tea. I was surprised to find joy in Pilates class, where I can focus my busy mind on the instructor's voice and move my bodymind in unison with my classmates. To be fully embodied helps me to trust what my bodymind knows, and this experience brings me deep joy and blesses my mental health. This is my truth: I deserve joy. We all deserve joy.

This morning, I get off the couch. I get myself another cup of coffee. I put on my favorite shirt. I find my fidget bracelets for extra comfort. I give myself permission to feel how I feel. It's okay to feel my feelings. I don't need to be ashamed of feeling tired. I won't feel this way forever. There is freedom, comfort, power, and hope in admitting the truth of the moment. To honor what is real empowers me to hope that things can change for the better.

Reflection Activity: Go outside or find a window to look out. Notice the color of the sky. What is the truth about how you are feeling today? What would happen if you were honest with yourself about it?

Prayer: God of hope, thank you for the truth of your love that sets me free. Amen.

With hope for today,
Pastor Sarah

Stillness

"Be still, and know that I am God!"—Psalms 46:10

One summer I was hiking in the White Mountains of New Hampshire with a friend. Our hike brought us to a very particular flat rock looking out over the surrounding mountains. Passing through a clearing of trees to this stunning cliff, it was as if the entire world had stopped. There were no cars or trains making busy noises. No cacophony of voices swirling nearby. Nothing on the calendar begging me to keep on the hamster wheel of work. The world was still. It was simply me, my good friend, God, a mild breeze, and all the green mountains one could see for miles. I stood there in awe for several minutes.

Awe is a gift. My mind began to heal, and I felt whole. I noticed my friend venture over near the edge, where there was a place to sit and soak in the view. I joined him, and while we talked a bit about our families, work, and *Star Wars*, we mostly sat in stillness. As we walked back down the trail, it occurred to me that eventually we all must come down off the mountain of stillness into real life. But even in "real life," the psalmist beckons us to be still. It is in the stillness that God meets us.

Stillness is always present, built into the fabric of existence. We feel the need to justify seeking stillness because it is unfairly perceived as laziness or weakness. But what if we valued tending to the stillness as much as tending to the working, doing, and achieving? I am not sure I realized how much my heart and bodymind needed to sit on the edge of the mountain. "Be still," God says, and in the stillness we will heal.

Reflection Activity: Find a quiet place to be in silence for as long as is comfortable, and pay attention to your breathing. Allow the stillness to ground you for whatever else comes in your day.

Prayer: When hope seems dim, O God, help me to be still long enough to awaken to your presence. Amen.

With hope for today,
Pastor Chad

Laugh

A time to weep, and a time to laugh; a time to mourn, and a time to dance.
—Ecclesiastes 3:4

Mental health fluctuates throughout the day. We can wake up feeling great, then by lunch be dropping into the pit of despair. We can laugh at breakfast, then cry in the bathroom by the end of the day. All of us experience the range of emotions described in Ecclesiastes, sometimes on the same day. Faith reminds us that God is with us, in the highs and in the lows, in the weeping and in the laughing, in the mourning and in the dancing.

Our family dog Fia is a medium-sized, black boxer-poodle mix. When she's outside chasing squirrels, she has this big smile on her face. Her eyes twinkle, and she makes a short, high-pitched bark. It's a full belly laugh: "Ha!"

We adopted a dog as the global pandemic dragged into its second summer in 2021. That first year of the pandemic brought two deaths in our family: my beloved ninety-nine-year-old grandmother from old age and my brilliant sixteen-year-old niece by suicide. Our hearts were ripped out of our chests; we were totally devastated. Talk therapy helped us in our grieving, but so did adopting a puppy.

I know firsthand the therapeutic value of having a pet. I am already planning each stage of life and what kind of pet will be needed given the level of loss involved. When I am an empty nester, I plan to get a teacup Yorkie (yes, you can judge me; I'm okay with it). It's sort of a family tradition. When I went off to college, as the youngest of five children, my mom replaced me with a long-haired miniature schnauzer named Shatzie. With the losses of life, we all need to find ways to laugh.

As your mental health fluctuates, what helps you to stay grounded? On a rough day, you may want to reach out to a friend, eat your favorite meal, move your bodymind in ways that feel good, watch your favorite show, talk to your therapist, or text/call 988 Lifeline for emotional support. Plan now for your hard days. What are three things you can do to feel better, and who are three people you can reach out to? Put this information somewhere you will see it often as a reminder.

Having a plan for what to do when I hit a rough patch with my mental health gives me hope and is empowering. Getting outside whenever I can and walking the dogs blesses my mental health. Weeping and mourning do not last forever. There is a time for laughter and rejoicing. All these feelings are part of what it means to be human.

Reflection Activity: Remember the last time you felt a laugh rising from inside of you. What does your laughter feel like? Can you also feel the joy Fia expresses when she barks her laughter?

Prayer: God of hope, may your Spirit bubble up from within me in the joy of laughter. Amen.

With hope for today,
Pastor Sarah

Wander

"Surely God has blessed you in all your undertakings; he knows your going through this great wilderness. These forty years God has been with you; you have lacked nothing."—Deuteronomy 2:7

I fear the unknown. Wandering around lost is a terrifying thought. I find myself significantly anxious when I do not know where I am going while driving somewhere new. Sometimes I rush decisions and run toward the things and places that feel safe. Thank God I am not alone in this struggle. The Israelites were known as a wandering and traveling community whose primary trust was in a God who promised to take them to a land flowing with milk and honey. God's covenant was tied to a promise to journey with them, and it was a matter of trust in God to follow the journey without exact coordinates or a clear plan of where they were going.

To wander is not a moral or spiritual failure, but a letting go of the need for certainty in faith. It is a reaching toward hope, toward a light when all seems dim. I love going out on a hiking trail and just wandering where I feel led to walk. It can be a little scary in parks or trails that I am unfamiliar with, but letting go of a need for a plan is a spiritual act of trust. God knew the wandering of the Israelites and provided for their every move. God knows when we have committed ourselves to going into the unknown and provides a way for us, just as God did for the Israelites.

Reflection Activity: The spiritual life is centered in faith, not certainty. In this spirit, go somewhere without a determined path and allow yourself to simply wander. Trust God with your unknown path today.

Prayer: When hope seems dim, O God, allow me to trust you as I wander into the unknown. Amen.

With hope for today,
Pastor Chad

Wonder

Pause and wonder! —Isaiah 29:9 (NKJV)

The most common cause of disability is depression. A retired minister once said to me, "I wonder what my life would have been like if I had not been able to get medication to help me with depression." Reading the Bible, praying, and going to church can help with some symptoms of depression, like feelings of despair and loneliness. But faith alone is not an antidepressant. It's okay to love Jesus and love your therapist. It's okay to take antidepressants and take your burdens to God in prayer. We can be faithful Christians and still experience depression.

For too long, the church has stigmatized mental health experiences. As a pastor with a history of depression and family members who live with chronic depression, I want you to know depression is not your "fault." There's nothing "wrong" with you. Depression is caused by complex combinations of environment, society, genetics, and history of trauma; most of these things are outside of your control. God loves people with depression.

I wonder what healing might be possible when the stigma and shame are lifted. I wonder what community we might find if we stop hiding depression in the shadows. There's no shame in taking mental health medication or going to therapy. God can work through meds and therapy, just as God can work through the Bible and prayer. I've benefited from professional mental health therapy for over twenty years, and I continue to experience profound levels of emotional and spiritual healing.

Recovery from complex post-traumatic stress disorder is lifelong, just as my faith formation is lifelong. I pause and give God thanks for God's faithfulness shown to me throughout my life by mental health professionals. I am filled with wonder at the unconditional love poured out in therapy sessions over the decades. My therapist blesses my mental health, and she is a witness to the work of God to bring healing in my life. I know this is true: hope comes in human form in compassionate and skilled therapists.

Reflection Activity: Take a moment to reflect on your own experiences with depression. Ups and downs are part of life, but prolonged periods of time (two weeks or more) of feeling down might be a sign that you could benefit from professional support. When was the last time you spoke with a mental health therapist and had a check-up from the neck up? God loves you, and you are worthy of care and support.

Prayer: God of hope, fill me with wonder at your love for me just as I am. Amen.

With hope for today,
Pastor Sarah

Faith

Now faith is the assurance of things hoped for,
the conviction of things not seen.—Hebrews 11:1

I am a person who wants a high probability of success before I enter something new. I do not need undeniable proof before I will believe something, engage in a project, or embrace another person's story. But it sure would help, right? It would help us to have some certainty as we journey through life, making decisions that impact ourselves and others, and as we discern how the Divine is speaking to us.

As I type this reflection, I am on an airplane, and I am trusting my very life to someone I have never met and who I assume has a pilot's license and has not had too much to drink. Trust is hard work, risky even, especially when you don't know someone or if you have experienced a particular trauma in life that makes it hard to trust others. Yet the author of Hebrews tells us that faith is, in fact, "the evidence of things not seen." The author reminds us that such faith goes before us in a cloud of witnesses.

Faith is also a radical living of hope, the "assurance of things hoped for." This is reassurance that God has already overcome all things, although we cannot see it yet. Have you experienced moments when the world seemed remarkably awful, gray, or dim, and you felt like giving up? Me too. My guess is the great cloud of witnesses felt like giving up too. Because we know God has provided for those who walked before us, we can be steadfast in our hope, trusting God even as we face the unknown.

Reflection Activity: Take out a piece of paper, voice recorder, or keyboard, and write responses to the following prompts. Where are you seeing hope in your week? List your own cloud of witnesses and how they have lived with faith. How are you holding onto hope with trust so defiant of what you see in the world that it almost seems foolish?

Prayer: When hope seems dim, O God, help me to endure my challenges and hardships in faith, knowing that you are always by my side. Amen.

With hope for today,
Pastor Chad

Accommodations

Hope deferred makes the heart sick, but a desire fulfilled is a tree of life.
—Proverbs 13:12

I find it helpful to have accommodations for my neurodiversity. These include fidgets, low overhead lighting, spaces of quiet, and the option to refrain from using technology. I have fidgets that are also prayer beads. When in a meeting with bright lights, I request for them to be dimmed if possible. When giving a presentation, I prefer not to use slide decks. If I become overstimulated by loud sounds, I seek a quiet, low-sensory space. I intentionally seek supportive, accommodating footwear because of special needs related to a foot injury from childhood. Instead of feeling ashamed or embarrassed about needing supportive shoes, I've learned to embrace it, and I seek colorful and playful options. This attitude boosts my mental health.

Accommodations are the things people need to be included, be involved, and belong. Accommodations make our communities accessible to all. Other examples include closed captioning, alternative seating options, elevator access, noise-cancelling headphones, large-print fonts, space to move around, the ability to take a mental health day, and alternative food options. Accommodations are not a burden but a joy because their presence means the whole body of Christ is being honored and supported. Offering and requesting accommodations expands and strengthens the bodymind of Christ. Normalizing accommodations is one way the church incarnates God's love, nurturing the tree of life.

I dream of a world where we begin with the assumption that most people would benefit from being offered accommodations. What if we provided a menu of accommodations as part of our community effort at inclusion? What if we offered everyone the opportunity to consider their needs for accommodations to remove barriers to belonging in every environment? There is no shame or stigma in asking for accommodations.

Reflection Activity*:* What accommodations benefit you or a loved one? Think about ways to make accommodations more accessible to people in your community. Today, be empowered to ask for what you need so you can truly belong in the spaces God is calling you.

Prayer: God of hope, help me be mindful of the need to advocate for accommodations today, for others and for myself. Amen.

With hope for today,
Pastor Sarah

Flourish

"The trees of God are watered abundantly, the cedars of Lebanon that God planted."
—Psalms 104:16

Just as the COVID-19 global pandemic was causing us all to shut down in March of 2020, a good friend gifted our family with a sugar maple tree to plant in our otherwise treeless backyard. By the time Earth Day approached, we had spent months in lockdown trying to tend to the challenges with faithfulness and compassion. Frankly, we were deflated, experiencing grief, and outright exhausted. It was a lot. My wife and I decided we had spent enough time indoors and needed to get outside to connect with the earth. We were struggling and needed to come alive. So, on Earth Day in 2020, we planted our sugar maple. Each of us took a turn digging, getting our hands dirty, and placing the tree in the earth. Sugar maples are not fast-growing; it will be years before we see a fully grown tree. But just because we can't see it does not mean the tree isn't flourishing.

Flourishing requires a community of nurture. Our family planted the tree with love, watered it, cut back some of the weeds and seedlings around it, and placed a stake with twine on it to hold the trunk so it could grow properly. The earth also helped this tree to flourish with the sun, nutrients of the soil, and rain. Now, several years later, the tree has already begun to flourish, showing strong growth, full leaves, and a beautiful shape.

Flourishing is not a solo experience, nor is it instantaneous. Flourishing is a process of growth in connection with a community of others who grow alongside us. Some refer to this as "shalom." The psalmist expresses human flourishing through the image of the trees God has planted. God helps trees to flourish just as God helps us to do the same.

Reflection Activity: What are the nutrients helping you to flourish in your mental health and in your faith? Are the nutrients rest or spiritual companions, healthy eating, or possibly discovering a new form of spiritual practice? Find those forms of spiritual practice that can give you the most growth, and let them nurture you today.

Prayer: When hope seems dim, O God, draw me toward that which helps me thrive and flourish. Amen.

With hope for today,
Pastor Chad

Joy

"I have said these things to you so that my joy may be in you, and that your joy may be complete."—John 15:11

Baptized as an infant in the Lutheran church, in my earliest faith formation as a child I got the impression that church was a serious matter and faith was joyless. There was a lot of sad organ music. No clapping. God was a white guy with a beard sitting up in the sky on a throne of clouds. Today I have come to appreciate the faith of my Lutheran friends and the beauty of organ music, and my images of God are much more diverse. But as a little kid, it wasn't obvious to me how the Christian faith made life better, let alone more joyful. Did God really want me to be joyful? Not all churches are the same. After my parents' divorce, my family started attending a new church, Broadway Christian Church (Disciples of Christ) in Columbia, Missouri. This church, its people, and their pastors, were joyful!

I had a childhood friend named Joy, a classmate in fourth grade at Fairview Elementary. Joy had curly, long, and thick brown hair. She wore big, brightly colored cable-knit sweaters, and her smile was contagious. I always wondered how much of her personality was shaped by her name: Joy.

Unlike Joy, who seemed to be living her best life each day, I was trying to figure out how to make new friends after moving across the country because of my parents' broken marriage. I wanted to be like Joy, but joy was hard to find. I felt sad.

After school, I'd come home to do my paper route, start homework, make ramen for dinner, do more homework, and go to bed. We were on food stamps and free lunch because my mom's public school teaching salary didn't provide enough for her and us five kids to get by. We were lucky to have extended family able to provide us modest housing, and I am grateful we were not unhoused, but times were hard.

Where was the joy in this very difficult period in my childhood? Later that school year, I made a new friend. Her name was Sarah, same as mine, and we formed a club at recess. It wasn't just any club, but a cheerleading club. We invented cheers and practiced our moves, and for ten minutes we were joy embodied. At recess I wasn't the poor kid; I was a cheerleader.

It's hard to experience joy when we feel cut off from other people or cut off from God. Part of the power of faith is that it connects us to others and to God. As a young adult, I prioritized working and accomplishing tasks instead of spending time with friends. But I often felt lonely. Now I make time each week to have tea with friends, helping me to feel more joyful and less lonely. This quality time in conversation with people I love improves my mental health. We are part of the beloved community, a fellowship of saints, both past and present. We are not alone. Joy comes in belonging. Joy comes in being known and loved. It's never too late to experience joy. This gives me hope.

Reflection Activity: The source of joy changes throughout the seasons of our lives. What brought you joy in your childhood? What brings you joy now? Write down the word "joy" on a sticky note or print it out. Stick it on or tape it to the bathroom mirror as a reminder to yourself that, though it may look different, joy can be found in every season of life.

Prayer: God of hope, bless my day with joyful moments when my spirit may be at ease. Amen.

With hope for today,
Pastor Sarah

Restore

You who have made me see many troubles and calamities will revive me again; from the depths of the earth you will bring me up again.
—Psalms 71:20

One of the most inspiring aspects of the life of Kentucky farmer, poet, and theologian Wendell Berry is that he farms in ways that restore the land from all the harm done to it by human beings. Humans have created harm through the pesticides we have used, mountaintop removal, and other forms of pollution. Berry is committed to sustainable practices and care of the land that embodies healing and restoration. This brings me hope. In one of his Sabbath poems, he calls us to restore the earth to what God intended. He writes:

> Leave your windows and go out, people of the world,
> go into the streets, go into the fields, go into the woods
> and along the streams. Go together, go alone.
> Say no to the Lords of War which is Money
> which is Fire. Say no by saying yes
> to the air, to the earth, to the trees,
> yes to the grass, to the rivers, to the birds
> and the animals and every living thing, yes
> to the small houses, yes to the children. Yes.—Wendell Berry[4]

The psalmist speaks about God bringing us up from our troubles and into a new and restored life. Whether going into the woods, into the fields,

[4] Wendell Berry, *Given: Poems* (New York: Catapult, 2006), 115.

into the classroom or the board room, to the pulpit or the world of transit, we all face situations that need restoration. How is God inviting you to live a life of hope and healing that helps bring restoration?

Reflection Activity: Wendell Berry suggests that this restored life requires saying no to the "Lords of War" and "Money" and saying yes to truly living with the earth. What do you need to say yes to today? What might living with the earth feel like, and how would it impact your mental health?

Prayer: When hope seems dim, O God, restore me within your creation and make me whole. Amen.

With hope for today,
Pastor Chad

Peace

May mercy, peace, and love be yours in abundance.
—Jude 1:2

Every Sunday in worship we have a "peace moment" where I lead the congregation in a communal time of silence. There's something powerful about being in community and creating space for listening to the holy. In the quiet, we attune our collective spirits to the One who is peace. I've learned to draw out the silence in worship to last longer than I am comfortable. Sometimes we can hear a bird singing outside the sanctuary windows; sometimes a child cries; sometimes I lose track of the time as I focus on my own breathing. It's countercultural to declutter our bodyminds and truly listen to the sounds within us and around us.

Of course, we don't have to be in worship to open ourselves to God's Spirit of peace because God's peace is always available to us, but worship helps us practice taking moments for peace in community with others. This might be the most meaningful part of worship for me: the peace moment. It's when the sounds of music and words fall away and our hearts are simply open to God. Hope sneaks into my heart in the peaceful stillness.

In the peaceful presence of the Holy One, I am embraced and held in God's compassionate love. I am reminded that I am connected to God and loved unconditionally. This spiritual practice of taking a moment of silence for peace helps to regulate my nervous system, creating a sense of well-being for my bodymind. Taking a moment to reflect on peace is good for my mental health.

I need the accountability of the gathered community to stay faithful to the practice of the peace moment. It helps to have other people with me. That's why I prefer yoga classes in person rather than by myself at home. It's wonderful to have the accessibility of online opportunities, but there is something different for me about being together in person. The regular practice of yoga helps me connect my faith to my bodymind. I often pray as I practice yoga. Sometimes my bodymind releases tears, and I feel deeply relaxed, allowing emotions to express themselves without words. The sense of abundant peace comes to me through the people around me; peace seems to be multiplied through our shared lives, in a shared space, in a shared time, in shared breath. We each manifest peace in our bodyminds. And peace multiplies, one person at a time. The ability for us to be people at peace, even for a few moments, brings me deep hope.

Reflection Activity: We start and end the peace moment in worship with the sound of a rain stick. Some people use the sound of a singing bowl, bells, or chimes. Try taking a moment today for silent reflection. In the silence, invite the peace of Christ to awaken hope within you.

Prayer: God of hope, when peace feels far away, hold me close in your love. Amen.

With hope for today,
Pastor Sarah

Connection

The eye cannot say to the hand, "I have no need of you," nor again the head to the feet, "I have no need of you."—1 Corinthians 12:21

I found myself in a small restaurant in Berea, Kentucky, one evening as I drove to this eclectic bluegrass town to accompany a colleague at a memorial service for a family member. The restaurant offers every noodle imaginable, with protein choices for everyone, and their hospitality and care for customers is way above average, coupled with small-town charm. The wall across from the entrance proclaims boldly: "WE BELONG TO EACH OTHER!" Below this message is an explanation of an organization or service project the restaurant supports. When you pay for your food, they ask if you want to give a tip to support the organization described on the wall. It might be digging wells in Africa, a women's shelter in Kentucky, or disaster relief in Appalachia. In 2016 alone, they gave away over forty thousand dollars to make the world a better place, all because they believe "we belong to each other."

This line—"We belong to each other"—is found in a famous quote from Mother Teresa: "If we do not have peace in this world, it is because we have forgotten that we belong to each other." We have long since forgotten our belonging and connection. We see so much fracture in the world, and this impacts our ability to live as whole people because it creates a terrifying loneliness.

Part of our emotional and spiritual well-being is establishing connection in a way that is life-giving. Paul understood the work of connection by drawing on the human body as an image, suggesting that what happens to one of us happens to all of us. We suffer and rejoice together. What a different world we would live in if you, as a foot, could say to me, as the hand, "I need you." Not only might we feel less lonely, but we would have the support we need to thrive.

Reflection Activity: What might connection feel like for you today? Though it may seem risky, move toward one person with whom your relationship needs nurturing and care.

Prayer: When hope seems dim, O God, help me to recognize my connection to all of your people and to celebrate the ties that bind us together. Amen.

With hope for today,
Pastor Chad

Silly

Rejoice in God always; again I will say, Rejoice.—Philippians 4:4

Being an aunt brings me joy. God's unconditional love for each of us is enough reason to rejoice always. No matter what else may be happening or the status of my mental health, I can rejoice in God's love for me. Being grounded in the love of God roots us in joy. One of my mental health spiritual practices is to embrace more joy in my life.

When I play with my nieces and nephews, I can get silly. In one day, I can easily switch from reading a scholarly theological book about Korean women in the morning to an afternoon playing with coloring books on the floor with markers. I believe I'm a better theologian because of these regular intervals of silliness and playfulness. The creativity connected to being silly is divine energy at work.

I'm trying to give myself more permission to be silly, even if my nieces and nephews are not around to play with. As I learn more about neurodiversity, I better appreciate how positive connections with others are strengthened through play. One gift neurodivergent people bring is their sense of playfulness and comfort with being silly, no matter their age!

Being silly can be a sacred act of honoring the divine spark within each of us. By not taking ourselves too seriously, we make room for the Spirit to take the lead. Silly balances out the sadness. We can give ourselves permission to experience moments of silliness in a world filled with hopelessness. My husband and I enjoy going on regular date nights, often including dinner and a show. We love live music, theater, and comedy shows because these environments invite a spirit of playfulness, excitement, and silliness. It's a great release of tension and stress to laugh, dance, and be moved by art. Creative performances also inspire me to imagine a more hopeful world. I feel a sense of unity when I am part of a group of people coming together in an audience to appreciate artistic expression.

Being silly and playful reminds me that rejoicing can sneak up on us. Rejoicing happens in between the tears. Hope has a way of breaking through.

Reflection Activity: Have you ever been in a group photo where the photographer says, "Now make a silly face!" What's your go-to silly face? Make a silly face now. Our bodyminds are in tune with the energy swirling all around us, and stress makes for tense bodyminds. Making a silly face helps break through the tension in our bodyminds. This can be a form of body prayer: make a silly face.

Prayer: God of hope, thank you for the silly ways I can express myself. Amen.

With hope for today,
Pastor Sarah

Dance

David danced before God with all his might; David was girded with a linen ephod. So David and all the house of Israel brought up the ark of God with shouting and with the sound of the trumpet.
—2 Samuel 6:14–15

I am blessed with a daughter who loves to dance. I still remember her first dance lesson at a local YMCA at the age of three. The teacher taught her how to flow with music, how to extend her legs out from her knee bone, how to hold the bar, and how to plié. The joy on my daughter's face was radiant. Over the years I've noticed dancers hold a delicate balance between following the patterns and craft of professional dancing and following the dance from within needing to be expressed.

David's dancing before God was driven from within during a very sacred moment in the life of the Israelites. Our lives can be more vibrant and hopeful when we allow ourselves to think of life as a dance, a flow of Spirit and energy that comes from God and lives within us to be creatively expressed into the world. While each of us may not physically be a dancer, we can invite the Spirit within to make our bones and spirits move, following God's lead. Each time I see my daughter dance, I can't help but smile seeing her joy and how the form of dance expresses who she is and how she feels.

We need spaces to express what lives inside of us. Sometimes we feel sad, depressed, angry, lonely, joyful, or even elated. All these emotions are valid. So the Spirit says, "Come and dance with me and open yourself to all that lives within you that longs to be expressed out into the world." Dance, dear ones, dance.

Reflection Activity: Engage with a piece of music, like jazz. Notice its creativity and celebrate its joy. What is it expressing? Or find your favorite song and allow yourself to dance to, move to, or feel its rhythm. Celebrate the way God has called you to uniquely and creatively express your life in the world.

Prayer: When hope seems dim, O God, let the music of this life sway us into your dance of love. Amen.

With hope for today,
Pastor Chad

Shadow

Yea, though I walk through the valley of the shadow of death, I will fear no evil; For You are with me; Your rod and Your staff, they comfort me.
—Psalms 23:4 (NKJV)

Psalm 23 is my favorite. The reference to the "shadow of death" has come to represent times I feel overwhelmed with sorrow, fear, dread, or despair. Psalm 23 reminds me I am not alone. God is with me and comforts me. This simple promise of God's loving presence is my salvation.

I can feel stuck in the shadows of my own mind. As a new mother with sleep deprivation, my anxiety took hold of me when I was afraid to sleep because what if my baby was hungry? Thankfully, extended family helped me get through this rough time. Sometimes we don't realize we are stuck in the shadows until after we come out and realize just how bad things had gotten.

This verse in Psalm 23 talks about the valley of the shadows, which is one of the most accurate descriptions in the Bible about mental health experiences of depression. The powerful and hopeful part of the psalm is the reminder that God is with us in the shadows to bring us comfort. It's important to understand that painful mental health experiences are not punishments from God, nor are they our fault because of lack of faith or because we have sinned. Our physical bodyminds, including our brains, experience changes that impact our mental health, such as the physical and emotional changes that accompany motherhood. God's love is with us, even in the shadows of our experiences.

I know that shadows will always be a part of my life because of who I am as a neurodivergent person. Neurodiversity is a word representing the diversity of ways people's bodyminds work. It is a form of self-identity, not a diagnosis, because there are a number of ways people are neurodiverse. Neurodiversity highlights the variation of our bodyminds and invites us to wonder instead of judging our differences. When we bring faith into conversations about mental health, we affirm that we can turn to God, family, friends, and therapists for support when we are stuck in the shadows.

Faith reminds us there is always light shining somewhere. Meeting with my spiritual director helps me navigate questions about where God is showing up in my life. She often asks thoughtful questions and guides me in exploring what gives meaning to my life. Especially when I am in a place of shadows, I need someone else to help me recognize the light.

Reflection Activity: Take time today to sit with a candle. This could be a battery-powered candle or one with a flame or another source of light or heat. Reflect on a time when you felt stuck in the shadows. Take this candle's light or warmth as a reminder of God's love for you. You are not alone.

Prayer: God of hope, thank you for being with me always, especially in the shadows. Amen.

With hope for today,
Pastor Sarah

Follow

"Whoever serves me must follow me; and where I am,
there will my servant be also.
Whoever serves me, God will honor."
—John 12:26

A common misconception is that there are leaders and followers and only those out front leading others are worthy of recognition or praise. The challenge with this logic is that it creates a hierarchy of worth, with not enough room for those who are leading to learn or grow alongside those who follow. There is little humility in this arrangement. Also, such models do not consider how mental health experiences such as anxiety, fear, depression, or ADHD might show up in this misconception of some people being worth more than others. We need a vision of leading and following that is grounded in service and compassion.

The movie *A Beautiful Day in the Neighborhood*[5] about the life of Fred Rogers contains a powerful scene where Mr. Rogers visits a person who is sick and near death. Near the end of their visit, Mr. Rogers whispers something into the ear of the man who is sick. The man replies, "You can count on it." Curious, one of the family members asks Mr. Rogers on his way out of the room what he said to the man.

Mr. Rogers replied, "I asked him to pray for me. I figure someone who is going through what he is going through must be awfully close to God." Fred Rogers was a well-known television figure, a public figure, and one many admired. While such adulation is meaningful, Mr. Rogers wasn't interested in being known for something or being famous as a leader. He humbled himself and asked a dying man to pray for him because he knew the man was close to God. He was not afraid to follow as well as lead. Fred Rogers was an example to us all of servant leadership.

Reflection Activity: If you are a leader, find someone you trust and try to follow them. If you are a follower, find a way to make yourself vulnerable and lead something challenging. Discuss with a friend or partner over lunch or tea how it felt to serve the world differently.

Prayer: When hope seems dim, O God, help me to say yes to following you. Amen.

With hope for today,
Pastor Chad

Witness

(Content Warning: Domestic Violence)

It is that very Spirit bearing witness with our spirit
that we are children of God.
—Romans 8:16

Getting ready one morning in my hotel room during a work trip, I heard muffled sounds of a conversation coming in through the bathroom vents. It sounded like two people having an argument. One person was speaking in a low voice, and the other person had a high voice and began to whimper. It was painful to hear. My heart went out to them. Something was not right.

I wondered, *Are they safe?* I tried to figure out if there was a way to check. What if I asked them through the vents if everything was okay? But then what if they yelled at me for eavesdropping? I decided to pray. I prayed for God's loving Spirit to be with them.

[5] *A Beautiful Day in the Neighborhood*, screenplay written by Micah Fitzerman-Blue and Noah Harpster, directed by Marielle Heller (Sony Pictures, 2019).

In graduate school, I worked for a domestic violence agency as a therapist for a support group. My hotel room neighbors' situation reminded me of what I had learned in my training about the power and control wheel. Even though I only heard snippets of the conversation, I had a hunch this behavior might be part of a larger pattern of emotional or physical domestic violence.

Sometimes we witness harm being done and we feel helpless to confront it. It is a reminder of the need for care, support, and love for people oppressed by violence. We need to advocate for more resources to help survivors and perpetrators of domestic violence. It takes courage to break the cycles of power, abuse, violence, and control. The Spirit connects us in love to one another as children of God. Also, some relationships need to change or come to an end.

I've learned to adjust my expectations of relationships in order to protect my own mental health, and this means giving permission to change how I relate to other people, especially if the relationship is not life-giving. Advocating for accountability in relationships is a form of love. The Spirit emboldens and empowers us to do so because *we* are *all* children of God, worthy of dignity, respect, and freedom from harm.

Reflection Activity: Reflect on a time when you have experienced the power of making a difference by being a witness. What happened and what did it feel like to be a witness?

Prayer: God of hope, when I witness something scary, bring your Spirit of protection over all who are in harm's way. Amen.

With hope for today,
Pastor Sarah

PS: Domestic violence does not discriminate and can impact anyone. If you or someone you know is impacted by domestic violence, there is help available at 1-800-799-SAFE.

Listen

My child, be attentive to my words; incline your ear to my sayings. Do not let them escape from your sight; keep them within your heart.
—Proverbs 4:20–21

Sometimes we allow ourselves to believe we are not enough. One evening, as I sat with my spouse mindlessly watching a television show after an exhausting week and feeling like I was in the shadows, I received a text message from a colleague and friend. We don't see each other or talk often. He is spiritual kin to me, though, and we thrive when we are together. We hadn't spoken in months when his text arrived: "Chad, just popped over here to say that you are more than your role, more than a position, and that you are more than enough just as you are. You are loved beyond measure for exactly who you are." Tears flowed from my eyes. How could he have known that this was a message I needed at that very moment?

I was struggling at the time with my sense of self-worth and impact, particularly as it related to how my work connects to the rest of my life. I couldn't believe how spot-on he was, so I asked him, "How did you know that is what I needed to hear?" His response was, "My friend, sometimes when we get quiet enough and listen, we can hear the Spirit speak to us." And there it was! In other words, I could have all the book smarts, say all the right things, and have many of the technical skills to be in my role, but the craft of attending to the Spirit is what reminds me I am enough. Perhaps you also know the struggle of self-worth all too well, and when that nagging voice in your head comes around to speak to you of unworthiness, there is hope in the pause, in attending deeply to the voice within you whispering, "You, dear one, are loved beyond measure for exactly who you are."

Reflection Activity: How do you attend to your inner voice? In whatever form that rises within you, take a moment in your day to be still and attend to the Spirit within your heart.

Prayer: When hope seems dim, O God, help me to quiet myself long enough to attend to what your Spirit is saying. Amen.

With hope for today,
Pastor Chad

Testimony

My mouth is filled with your praise, and with your glory all day long.
—Psalms 71:8

How does your life give praise to God? When we think about praising God, we often think about thanking God for all the blessings in our lives. But what if we could also praise God during the harder parts of life, too? Not because God made our lives hard to make us strong, but because God's love gets us through the hard times. We praise God for bringing us through the valley of pain and suffering. We praise God for getting us through the devastating depression, the chronic anxiety, and the overwhelming dread. For the moments of ease, for the moments of lightness, for the moments of joy, even fleeting flashes of grace, we give thanks to God. We praise God all day long for the love that blesses us as we live each day, one day at a time.

We know people often choose to stay home from church when they are not emotionally in a good place. One recent widow told me she wasn't ready to come to church because she wasn't "strong enough." She said she was afraid to cry at church. I reminded her it is okay with God and with us for her to cry at church. We missed her and wanted to be with her again. She's not the only person who has felt that way. How can the church be more welcoming to people experiencing emotional distress? What is your God story about mental health experiences? How does God manifest in your life? The stories we tell about how God is present with us are at the heart of our testimony. We testify to the power of God at work in our lives. Everyone has a story.

For me, sometimes it seems like God is very far away, if not totally absent from my life. I especially feel distant from God when I am stuck in the depths. Hope feels very far away. In times like these, it helps me to remember a time when God felt close by, a time when I felt loved by God, a time when I felt like God was with me.

Talk therapy sessions are times when I can tell stories about my life in a safe place without fear or judgment. I can be honest with myself and name things that are too big to keep trapped inside my head. In therapy, I can struggle out loud with my feelings of failure, feelings of inadequacy, and feelings of uncertainty. I also testify to my personal experiences of pain and suffering with a group of trusted friends on a regular prayer call. We hold space for one another to check in; then we pray for each other. This time together is a blessing to our mental health, encourages our faith, and instills in us hope, knowing we are not alone.

Sometimes my therapist witnesses my inner pain, and that is enough—to experience her affirmation of my feelings. Sometimes my therapist testifies to me, reminding me I am not alone: God is with me, God loves me, and God has plans to bless me. I am grateful for testimonies we can both give and receive as gifts. Through our testimonies, we are transformed by the power of God's love to save us from despair.

We testify to the power of God's love to reach us, especially when we are feeling emotional distress. Whether we are grieving the death of a loved one or the death of a dream, expressing these emotions is what can bring hope and healing. To be able to shed tears, to be able to share the stories, to be held with compassion, to be reminded that we are loved... these are the ways we offer praise all day long.

Reflection Activity: Have you ever thought about therapy as both witness and testimony? What would it feel like to share with your therapist how God is showing up in your life? If you don't have a therapist, find another safe person you can share your testimony with today.

Prayer: God of hope, for the testimony of all the saints reminding me of your love, I give thanks. Amen.

With hope for today,
Pastor Sarah

Gentleness

I, therefore, the prisoner in the Spirit, beg you lead a life worthy of the calling to which you have been called, with all humility and gentleness, with patience, bearing with one another in love, making every effort to maintain the unity of the Spirit in the bond of peace.

—Ephesians 4:1–3

When I think of living in gentleness, I think of my two great-grandmothers. They were pillars in my early life. One was a farmer and the other an educator, and I believe these vocations shaped how they related to their great-grandchildren. The patience it takes to let things grow in fields and to rely on weather patterns to sustain life is formative to spiritual life. The grace and resilience required to sit with children and ensure they are well taught and listened to is a gift beyond measure to the spiritual path. These were my great-grandmothers through and through: patient, filled with grace, and resilient. They grew up in the years of the Great Depression, bearing witness to hardship, and their capacity to help me navigate the struggles of my early years was grounded in a gentleness of spirit that lingers with me still.

I recall my great-grandmothers' compassionate way of speaking to me, even when they needed to say something difficult. Their words were soft, caring, and grounded in loving me just as I was at the time. When I made mistakes, they gently helped me to own them and move quietly toward a new way of living. When I struggled with feeling sad or with my mental health, they listened with love.

Perhaps when you hear these words from Ephesians, people come to mind who embody them in your life. They may be family members, friends, colleagues, or mentors. Their living gently on the earth and with others is a reminder of the calling to live with gentleness. In a world defined by harsh criticism, a rough exterior, or a hardness of heart, what a difference gentleness can make. If I could live even a fraction of the gentleness of Gladys and Cecil, my great-grandmothers, I'd at least be moving toward the vision of scripture. I invite you to come alongside those whose footprints are grounded in gentleness.

Reflection Activity: Pause briefly, and with your inhale and exhale, bring to your mind's eye those in your life who have modeled the path of gentleness. Once you have brought them to your mind, give God thanks for them and their witness in your emotional and spiritual journeys. If they are still living, take the time to thank them for their gentleness.

Prayer: When hope seems dim, O God, may your gentleness live within me as it has lived so beautifully in those who have traveled the road of faith and mental health before me. Amen.

With hope for today,
Pastor Chad

Missing

"Collect all who seem like they need a square meal, all the misfits and homeless and down-and-out you can lay your hands on, and bring them here."
—Luke 14:21 (MSG)

Once a person lovingly described their church as the "island of misfit toys." In the gospels, Jesus offers an extravagant welcome to people society casts aside and leaves behind. Anyone who has ever felt forgotten and dismissed can relate to the feeling of being unlovable. I imagine that's how the misfits, unhoused, and down-and-out people in this gospel story felt. This is how I sometimes felt as a child.

On a family road trip when I was a child, we stopped at a gas station and all got out of the RV. As the youngest of five children, I often followed my older siblings around. I remember wandering around the gas station convenience store and suddenly becoming aware of my surroundings and feeling scared. Where did everyone go? I started to cry.

"Are you missing?" a kind store clerk asked. They brought me up to the check-out counter and had me sit next to them on a bar stool. My family was gone. Back in the RV, headed down the highway an hour later, my mother says, "Has anyone seen your little sister?" Silence. The RV stopped and turned around.

When my family found me, I was standing outside the convenience store with an ice cream cone. It was scary to be left behind, but I am grateful for the kindness of the store clerk who took care of me. Today I am grateful to have a faith community that reminds me I belong to the family of God.

We share hope when we extend an extravagant welcome to anyone seeking belonging. Community doesn't need to be perfect to create a sense of belonging, but it does need to be a place where people can be their authentic selves. Belonging means you are missed if you are not present. I am part of a monthly dinner group of friends. We look forward to these dinners to spend time in conversation, catching each other up on how our families are doing and how we are navigating being ministers, wives, and mothers. When one of us can't make it to dinner, we reschedule because it's important for us all to be there. When one of us is missing, things just are not the same. We all need places where we are missed when we are not there because we belong.

Reflection Activity: Reflect on a place you belong where you would be missed if you weren't present?

Prayer: God of hope, show me who is missing from the table, and help me extend an invitation. Amen.

With hope for today,
Pastor Sarah

Heal

"Come to me, all you that are weary and are carrying heavy burdens, and I will give you rest."—Matthew 11:28

I see our neighbor Mark pulling a red wagon behind him from down the street. This is a daily ritual for Mark, as he pulls Silas for his daily walk. One of several rescue basset hounds in Mark's care, Silas' back legs do not work, yet he loves to go on walks. Mark places little mittens on his feet so that when Silas gets out of the wagon to "walk," his feet won't scrape on the sidewalk. Mark and his family work with a local rescue to host basset hound dogs in hospice care or those that will not be taken by others because of traumatic injury or disability. Unfortunately, owners abandon dogs that do not conform to the typical dog's ability, and dog rescues are left with very few options for caring for them.

Healing of the world occurs when people like Mark offer care for those who cannot care for themselves. I know many caregivers whose lives resemble this kind of compassion and care. Silas' physical ailments may never heal, but Mark is playing a part in mending and making whole not only Silas' life, but the whole of creation. When Jesus says, "Come to me, all that are weary and are carrying heavy burdens, and I will give you rest," Jesus is addressing a deeper sense of woundedness and weariness we all experience. Jesus offers rest from these wounds and Jesus provides us with the comfort we all long for deep within.

We all have wounds to heal from, and sometimes we need others to pull the red wagon and help us heal. We need others with the kind of compassion Mark offers. We need healing from the harsh world that would rather abandon us and leave us for dead. Loneliness and depression can be a crushing reality, so when Jesus offers us rest, he does so not because all the pain will magically go away, but because Jesus knows that healing is not always obvious. Healing requires a daily tending to our wounds and the wounds of the world with love, rest, and compassion. May it be so for you today.

Reflection Activity: Take ten minutes to journal and reflect on what wounds need tending in your journey. If you have trust in a deep and abiding friendship, ask that person to help hold the pain with you. Then release it to God and allow God's love to be the salve that helps you to heal.

Prayer: When hope seems dim, O God, may I find deep rest within you. May your healing bind up my wounds and give me peace. Amen.

With hope for today,
Pastor Chad

Soft

"I will not leave you orphaned; I am coming to you."—John 14:18

The gospel of John tells the story of God's abiding love for us. God desires a relationship with us and desires to nurture us in the heart of divine love. This feminine, soft form of mothering spiritual love is a gift we receive from God. We can embrace experiencing God's soft love and comfort, allowing us to be filled with the nourishment of God's grace and mercy. Prayer is a portal, opening our hearts to welcome in the love of God.

Finding comfort during days that are hard for our mental health sometimes means finding sensory or tactile reassurances like a soft blanket, soft clothing, soft fidgets, soft and quiet environments, and soft lighting. On harsh days when the world is loud in my head, I can find better regulation of my emotions by seeking out things that are soft. I like to have soft items at my desk when I am working, soft items in the car when I am driving, and soft textures in my purse accessible to me wherever I am.

Recovery from complex post-traumatic stress disorder (CPTSD) means that I use accommodations to help me day-to-day. Soft textures are part of my recovery. There is nothing to be ashamed about when it comes to accommodations. Everyone has the right to have their accommodation needs met.

Some people prefer textures other than soft. What is important is to be open to exploring whatever works best for you. I also like to use calming strips, which are available in multiple textures and colors. These are textured stickers you can use to provide the sensation that is most beneficial to you. I have a calming strip on my cell phone that reminds me to "inhale" and "exhale." As a highly sensitive person, I often feel emotions physically, such as a headache, upset stomach, or tightness in my neck and shoulders. Trusting my body, honoring what it is telling me, listening to my bodymind, then taking care of my bodymind are ways I support positive mental health. Comforting myself with soft textures is an important way for me to honor my bodymind.

Reflection Activity: What soft item might you engage with today that can bring you comfort? Find a soft pillow, blanket, or other item that you can use to intentionally experience the soft texture of the material. When we use multiple senses, we remind ourselves that God created us to experience the comfort that softness brings. Make time for self-soothing today.

Prayer: God of hope, thank you for the gift of softness that comforts me. Amen.

With hope for today,
Pastor Sarah

Strength

But I will sing of your might; I will sing aloud of your steadfast love in the morning. For you have been a fortress for me and a refuge in the day of my distress.—Psalms 59:16

I look out upon a sea of seven hundred people in a cold middle school gym, and I see Ken's face in the back. My dear friend had come to support me. One of the most challenging funerals I have ever done was for a twelve-year-old boy who was hit by a truck while riding his bicycle to school. I had led funerals for elderly people and those who spent years slowly dying of cancer, but never for a tragedy of this nature and certainly not with one so young. I knew if I was going to offer a comforting presence at that moment, I would need a strength beyond my own.

The memorial service for the community was at the middle school where he was a student. I had never been asked to comfort seven hundred people like that, and I was scared. Knowing me as well as he did, my good friend called to check on me several times the week before the service, and somehow he knew I needed his support without me needing to ask. Looking across that middle school gym and seeing Ken's familiar and comforting face was the sort of strength I needed to be grounded for such a moment. His friendship was God's gift to me, reminding me I was not alone.

There is a hubris to the notion that we can do things on our own, isolated and apart from God and others. The theology claiming we must pull ourselves up by some sort of spiritual bootstraps is akin to the idolatry of the Israelites seeking their own gods instead of relying upon God to lead them through the wilderness.

Where will you derive your strength today? Know that you can call on God, and then, along with the psalmist, you can sing of the strength God provides. Know that there is also a refuge of strength in the "Kens" in your life. You don't have to face whatever you are going through alone.

Reflection Activity: Who might be a friend you can call upon and trust they will respond? Our strength is not based on doing hard things alone but is intertwined with the community that surrounds us.

Prayer: When hope seems dim, O God, let me lean on the strength that you provide. Amen.

With hope for today,
Pastor Chad

Cozy

I am confident of this, that the one who began a good work among you will bring it to completion by the day of Jesus Christ.
—Philippians 1:6

The drive for perfectionism is often at the root of self-loathing. Striving to make everything we do, how we look, our professional lives and personal lives perfect... to strive for perfection is exhausting. I am a three on the enneagram, which means I am constantly striving to achieve at the highest level possible. I want success. I want to reach my goals. And I want the world to know because I want to be appreciated for how hard I work. I am set up to fail because no matter how hard I strive, I will never be perfect all the time. That's humanly impossible. I desperately need reminding of scripture's emphasis on the lifelong process of becoming "complete" rather than becoming "perfect."

I find hope in the concept of lifelong learning and growth. We can be cozy with who we are right now, while also affirming God's good work in us is a lifelong process. It's not about winning the life achievement award. It's about our failures and what we learn from our mistakes along the way. I can be confident in God's love for me, not only when I fail and fall short of meeting my goals, but especially when I fall down. I can be confident in God's unconditional love.

During my sabbatical in the summer of 2023, I listened to Beyoncé's *Renaissance* album on repeat. Her song "Cozy" is an anthem of colorful language for people like me in recovery from trauma. The line that says it all is this one: "She's a hero, survived all she's been through ... comfortable in my skin, cozy with who I am."[6] For months I played "Cozy" on repeat loud in my car and sang at the top of my lungs.

It's easy to internalize messages that degrade and devalue us. Whether the hurtful words and actions are directed at us by bullies or come from the discrimination all around us in a society that questions our worth,

[6] "Cozy," by Beyoncé, Honey Redmond, Christopher Lawrence Penny, et al., track 2 on *Renaissance* (Parkwood Entertainment/Columbia Records, 2022).

it is an act of faith to proclaim we are worthy of God's love. It is an act of love to be "cozy" with who we are. As a woman, it takes courage to be cozy in our bodminds because of the unrealistic pressure to look young and flawless. Instead of ignoring my bodymind, as a form of detached disassociation, as my mental health improves, I've started taking better care of my skin by using sunscreen daily. This may seem obvious, but for a long time I didn't think I deserved to wear sunscreen every day. Now, I put on face lotion at night and in the morning, each time using this ritual as a blessing to honor the divine within.

To be cozy with who we are means we can let our guard down in our own skin. We can breathe with our whole bodmind. We can feel safe enough to close our eyes. We can turn off the fight, flight, flee, or fawn response to danger, our finely honed hypervigilance survival strategy. God's Spirit can ease our bodyminds for a moment. Cozy is a spiritual practice.

Reflection Activity: God loves you just as you are right now. Do you believe this good news? Getting cozy with who we are is part of the life of faith. What helps you feel cozy? Give yourself permission to create rituals to enhance your sense of being cozy in God's love.

Prayer: God of hope, help me to be cozy in my own skin. Amen.

With hope for today,
Pastor Sarah

Lost

"Those who find their life will lose it, and those who lose their life for my sake will find it."—Matthew 10:39

We often think of the word "lost" as negative. We take a couple of wrong turns driving, and the next thing we know, we are lost. Or an important family heirloom got packed away in a box, and later when unpacking, cannot be found. But what if being "lost" can bring us closer to the Divine? What if we were to think of it as getting lost in the music or lost as immersion in a breathtaking view? Being lost in this sense moves us from mundane reality and into the presence of God, where all boundaries of time seem to disappear. With all we have swirling in our bodyminds and stress, expectations, and pain in the world, we desire to find ourselves lost in the wonder of the Divine, lost in hope.

In the last few years, thanks to a dear friend, I began learning the art of stained glass. One of the blessings of this long and slow craft is that I can find myself lost in my studio without realizing how many hours have passed. There is a sense that I have entered another realm. My headspace clears, and all my worries, fears, and anxieties take a vacation for a bit while I center my attention and gaze to the colors and shapes before me.

I love getting lost in this art because it allows my heart and head to heal, my speed of life to slow down, and my sense of purpose to become clearer. The mental health experiences of my daily life have some breathing space to be creative and explore new spaces. When I find myself lost in art, my sense of identity as an individual becomes threaded through the life of the Divine, losing my life to find it.

Reflection Activity: What might you find yourself getting lost in today? Let go of the fast-paced demands of your day, even if just for a bit, and allow yourself to get lost in a life-giving activity to heal, restore, refocus, and connect with God and yourself again.

Prayer: When hope seems dim, O God, help me to let go and get lost in your love so that I may be found again. Amen.

With hope for today,
Pastor Chad

Openness

"Ask, and it will be given you; search, and you will find; knock, and the door will be opened for you."—Matthew 7:7

Mental health episodes often feel like a door slammed shut in your face. Panic attacks prevent you from going out. Irritable bowel syndrome activated by anxiety and stress slows you down. A major depressive episode closes you off from communicating with those you love. Imagine God giving us the care we need, finding the self-esteem we have lost, and opening the door to recovery.

Prayer connects us to a God who cares about these things. God desires for each of us to experience abundant life, our daily bread. This includes those of us who live with mental health experiences that impact our lives and the lives of people we love daily.

I was thirty years old when my dad died from decades of neglecting his health because of his untreated bipolar disorder. My grief created an openness for healing. As I've tried to make sense of his death, I've longed to better understand how his condition complicated our relationship as father and daughter. My whole life, his mental health was in crisis, with extreme highs and lows. I did not ever know my father when he lived with positive mental health.

In seeking to heal from the loss of the relationship I desired with my father, I longed for grace and forgiveness. I realized the anger, hurt, fear, and disappointment I carried toward my father were not serving me well. I was surprised by God's Spirit of openness that landed in my heart. This spiritual openness invited me to let go of the anger, to let go of the hurt, to let go of the fear, to let go of the disappointment.

I did not know it was possible to heal a relationship with someone who is dead. Openness makes healing possible. I am still healing. One of the most healing places for me is the ocean. My mother lives by the beach, and whenever I visit her, I look forward to morning beach walks. Walking on the beach along the water's edge calms my nervous system. I tune into the sound of the waves washing onto shore, the sound of seabirds, the feeling of the breeze, the smell of the salt air, and the feeling of the warmth of the sun. All these sensory experiences affirm my sense of being alive in the present moment, and everything good seems possible. Praise God for the Spirit who can make new life rise from the dead.

Reflection Activity: Where in your life could a spirit of openness bring you healing? Is there a relationship in your life that is weighing you down? Pray today for God's Spirit to create in your heart an openness for letting go of all that harms you in body, mind, and spirit.

Prayer: God of hope, make a pathway for openness as I seek to be free from all harm.

With hope for today,
Pastor Sarah

Found

"Then the parent said to the child, 'Child, you are always with me, and all that is mine is yours. But we had to celebrate and rejoice, because this sibling of yours was dead and has come to life; they were lost and have been found."
—Luke 15:31–32

Panicked, my daughter came running into the living room shouting, "I can't find Jimmy! I can't find Jimmy!" In her young world, this was a huge tragedy. Jimmy is one of the stuffed animals she has had since birth, a fluffy wrapping of love each day and a comfort at bedtime when she is afraid of the dark. He was nowhere to be found. Our daughter had just visited my parents' house, so we checked in there. We looked furiously in each room of our house. Our panic and laser focus in our search for this lost item was unparalleled. Looking back, I cannot recall where we found Jimmy, but I do remember the relief and peace we felt when we finally found him. We could all relax, or we felt like throwing a party. All for a stuffed animal. I understand the father in Luke 15 rejoicing when someone he loved had been found.

Few of us will experience the profound sense of losing a child. However, we will lose many other things that need to be found again. Perhaps we lose our sense of purpose and struggle to find it again, or perhaps we lose a friendship in need of repair or clarity. We may lose confidence. In some cases, we may lose a sense of hope. The feeling of panic makes sense for such losses, and there is no magic answer for finding these things. The parent from the gospel of Luke demonstrates this in their willingness to be patient and wait for that which needed finding, even amid the panic. I imagine the parent was worried, panicked, and freaking out. I would be. I am inspired by the parent's willingness not to ignore the panic, but rather to insist that there is still hope in the middle of it all.

Reflection Activity: How can you be attentive to that which is lost within you or around you with patience and resilience? Design a party that you will throw when whatever is lost is, indeed, found in your life. Invite a friend to join you in celebrating the joy of that which is found, and give God thanks together.

Prayer: When hope seems dim, O God, may I throw a party for that which is found. Amen.

With hope for today,
Pastor Chad

Embrace

A time to throw away stones, and a time to gather stones together; a time to embrace, and a time to refrain from embracing.
—Ecclesiastes 3:5

On my home refrigerator is a large magnet depicting thirty emojis expressing different emotions. There is a floating magnet frame that can be moved around, highlighting whatever feeling the viewer is drawn to. I like to highlight "hopeful." If I were more honest, I would also put the frame around the crabby face and tired face more often. But I highlight the feeling I wish I felt instead: hopeful. I think, *Maybe if I highlight this feeling, then I will start to feel this way.* But that's not how emotions work. I'm working with my therapist on being okay with the full spectrum of my feelings, especially the ones I've been taught to suppress, like rage, fear, disgust, and discomfort.

When I was growing up, my family did not openly and honestly express our emotions to one another. We also did not show affection, like giving hugs. We did not say "I love you." As Ecclesiastes says, "we refrained from embracing"—except it wasn't a season; it was a lifetime. Until it wasn't.

In my senior year of high school, I remember going to a professional photo session for the new church directory. By that time, it was just me and my mom, with four older brothers and a sister who were out of the house, off to college. I'll never forget standing with my mom, the photographer directing us to stand closer together. He directed me to put my hand on my mother's shoulder.

At that moment, I realized this stranger was making us do something unfamiliar. I've reflected on this moment many times. As I got older, with the help of my therapist, I realized I could change this multigenerational pattern of behavior that came from my mother's mother, who also didn't hug and didn't say "I love you." It's not because they aren't loving people; quite the opposite: it just wasn't part of my family's German and English cultures.

Today I embrace my mother and say "I love you." I embrace my child and tell him "I love you." I discovered how to change family patterns of behavior. The season for refraining from embracing came to an end with my generation. I find hope in the ways our family has broken unhealthy cycles, such as withholding affection. I enjoy connecting with my mother now as I get older, and we both treasure our regular phone conversations, where I always end the phone call with these words: "I love you, Mom."

Reflection Activity: What is the culture of embracing in your family? Do you wish it were different? Think of a time when an embrace felt good. Wrap your arms around yourself, and hold yourself in a tender, loving embrace. Know that God loves you.

Prayer: God of hope, help me to embrace what needs embracing and to let go of that which no longer blesses me. Amen.

With hope for today,
Pastor Sarah

Sacred

I praise you, for I am fearfully and wonderfully made. Wonderful are your works; that I know very well.
—Psalms 139:14

Like so many, I grew up singing the hymn "Amazing Grace" and hearing those famous words: "a wretch like me." While I do not deny there is sin or evil in the world, I have seen the devastating impact of a theology that begins with depravity and naming us as "wretches." I have seen such theology enable shame to permeate lives, leading to harmful outcomes not only in how we relate to other human beings, but also in how we relate to God and ourselves. Such a negative view of human nature plays into the stigma related to mental health experiences and our sense of worthiness. I long for a day when we can break free from such stigma. I can't help but think that things could be different if our starting spirituality is one where we affirm our sacred worth and our belovedness.

Indiana folk singer Carrie Newcomer's poem "Showing Up" begins with these words: "You / Are holy / And sacred / And utterly unique. / There are gifts you were born to give. / Songs you were born to sing / Stories you were born to tell. / And if you do not give it, / The world will simply lose it."[7] What if this sense of being sacred was our beginning point? Yes, you, dear reader, are utterly unique and absolutely sacred, and you have gifts and songs and stories to offer this blessed world.

The psalmist says, "I praise you, for I am fearfully and wonderfully made" (Ps. 139:14). What a wonderful starting point for describing who God has made you to be. Perhaps you need a reminder today of your sacredness. Perhaps you are called to remind others of their sacredness today. In moments when the voices of the world speak of how unworthy you are, what a wretch you are, how weak you are because you experience depression, how much you lack, or what you have not yet accomplished according to some impossible standard, remember that you are holy and sacred and utterly unique just as you are.

Reflection Activity: Let your story rise to be shared. Let your gifts be opened so that others may receive who God has made you to be. Whether that is writing a poem, painting a canvas, playing an instrument, or writing a song, your stories and gifts matter. Or you can share the gift of friendship by enjoying the company of a loved one. Enjoy the gift of nature and bask in the warmth of the sun. You are enough. You are, yes, imperfect and yet whole. Repeat this mantra: *I am a beloved child of God.*

Prayer: When hope seems dim, O God, remind me that I am sacred, that I am fearfully and wonderfully made. Amen.

With hope for today,
Pastor Chad

Warmth

This is what I have seen to be good: it is fitting to eat and drink and find enjoyment in all the toil with which one toils under the sun the few days of the life God gives us; for this is our lot.—Ecclesiastes 5:18

The author of Ecclesiastes says it like it is: life can be hard. That doesn't mean life will always be hard. This is important to remember when we are overwhelmed with our mental health. Whether it's taking care of

[7] Carrie Newcomer, *A Permeable Life: Poems and Essays* (Available Light Publishing, 2013), 16.

your own well-being or caregiving for the well-being of a loved one, we all deserve moments of enjoyment.

The warmth of the sun. The warmth of a cup of tea. The warmth of a blanket. The warmth of a bath. The warmth of a dog sitting at your feet or a pet curled up in your lap. The warmth of a loved one's hand in yours. I seek warmth to help calm my mind. When I am feeling overwhelmed, anxious, uncertain, and tired, the feeling of warmth comforts me. I always keep a fuzzy blanket nearby, in every room in my home and at work.

There are simple things we can do to help bring ease and relaxation to our nervous system. Weighted blankets or heating pads can help us to regulate and to know we will be okay. There is nothing shameful about needing help. It's okay to seek warmth when your bodymind is feeling stressed. You deserve warmth and compassion.

We can feel guilty experiencing pleasure amid suffering. We may question whether we deserve to feel good. We worry the enjoyment is fleeting, fearing disaster is fast on its way, so we are not fully present to experience pleasure. This is where mindfulness and being here, right now, in this moment is an act of courageous hope. One way I wrap myself in warmth is by floating in warm water, either a heated swimming pool or a warm bath. Floating in warm water recreates a feeling of being nurtured in the womb, and it is like a hug for my soul.

Wrap yourself in the warmth of God's love. You are enough. You are worthy of experiencing pleasure and comfort.

Reflection Activity: Make some time today for warmth. What simple ways can you bring warmth to your nervous system, reminding yourself of what fourteenth-century Christian mystic Julian of Norwich said: "All shall be well, and all shall be well, and all manner of things shall be well."[8]

Prayer: God of hope, bless me with warmth today as a sign of your grace. Amen.

With hope for today,
Pastor Sarah

Call

As Jesus went from there, he saw two other brothers, James son of Zebedee and his brother John, in the boat with their father Zebedeee, mending their nets, and he called them. Immediately they left the boat and their father, and followed him.—Matthew 4:21–22

When I was pastor of a local church, one of my parishioners worked as a hairdresser in a nearby retirement home. She talked about all the military veterans who came to sit in her chair and all the wartime stories that came

[8] Julian of Norwich, *Revelations of Divine Love*, chap. 27.

pouring out. Given all the trauma they had experienced, her chair was one of the only places the veterans felt safe to share their story.

One night she decided to ask the veterans to come to her studio and share their stories with one another. Through many tears, much of what had been buried deep within themselves came out into the world. Healing began to flow. I told my parishioner, "This is ministry! You are answering your call." She insisted, "No, no, I am not called. Ministry is what you do, pastor."

We have this notion that only those who answer a call to church ministry are ministers. I gently reminded her that she, too, was answering a call by offering a safe and sacred space for the wounds of war to heal among veterans. I am not sure I convinced her she had been called or that this was ministry. But I believe every single one of us is called because we all have a purpose: whether as a hairdresser, a teacher, an engineer, a business owner, a coach, a mentor, a parent, a writer, a realtor, a physician, a mental health therapist, a farmer, or even a pastor. Jesus called the disciples and calls you, too.

Reflection Activity: Sit down over coffee or tea with a trusted friend and discuss the idea of calling as your life purpose. What gift do you have to give the world that needs nurturing as a call? How might your friend see that gift within you?

Prayer: When hope seems dim, O God, help me to answer your call, even in your smallest of whispers. Amen.

With hope for today,
Pastor Chad

Depth

These things God has revealed to us through the Spirit; for the Spirit searches everything, even the depths of God.—1 Corinthians 2:10

I once thought my faith was lost in the depths of the sea. At the age of eighteen, the summer after high school graduation, I stared into the English Channel and felt totally lost. God felt very far away, and depression sank deep into my soul. I stared into the dark waters and saw nothingness. I lost God to the depths.

What I realize looking back at that time in my life is that I desperately needed therapy, but I had no clue. I didn't know there was help for the kind of problems I faced at home with my parents' divorce and my father's symptoms of bipolar disorder. I wish an adult had reached out to me during my teenage years to connect me with professional mental health support for my depression. Instead, I lost connection to hope and felt utterly alone. It was a difficult time in my life.

I found a letter from my brother Steve written to me during this time in my life. He said that he saw I was suffering emotionally with depression, and he wished I could get some help. It turns out wishing doesn't make a thing happen. There was no adult in my life who could advocate for me to get mental health support. Going to church was the closest thing to therapeutic support I experienced because of the community of caring people who welcomed me.

I've been lost in the depths of despair. Thanks be to God for the miracle of not falling headfirst into the sea forever and never returning to dry land. I am still here. The depth did not overcome me. I give thanks for the faith community that sang songs of hope over me, even when I didn't have the strength or desire to sing them for myself.

When God's presence feels far away, the depths can be a scary place. When God's presence is known in the depths, we are held in the depth of God's love. As an adult, I can advocate for my own mental health, and I have benefited from decades of therapy. Through years of regular talk therapy, I rediscover God again and again in the depths of life. In between my therapy sessions, I seek healing in nature and talk to the trees. There's a nature center within walking distance of my home, and one of my favorite ways to relax and give myself a natural mental boost is to sit in the nature center garden next to a big tree. I feel connected to myself and to God in this sacred space in nature.

Caring for our mental health is a way to connect to the Spirit. The Spirit reminds us of our connection to God. This connection can save our lives, especially when we feel lost and alone in the depths of life.

I encourage you to get a check-up from the neck up. Seek professional counseling support for yourself and your loved ones. Just as we normalize routine dental care and promote dental hygiene, we can treat care for our mental health the same way. Let's normalize mental health screenings, treatment, and therapy. Too many people are lost in the depths, and we don't even realize it. We can reach them before it is too late. It starts with connecting everyone with quality mental health services. Mental health care is a God-given right. We all deserve to enjoy positive mental health.

Reflection Activity: Reflect on what emotions within you could benefit from professional counseling help in order to heal.

Prayer: God of hope, thank you that you never let me go, even when I feel lost in the depths of life. Amen.

With hope for today,
Pastor Sarah

PS: If you or a loved one is feeling stuck, overwhelmed, or caught in the depths of depression or other emotions, there is help. You can call or text the 988 Lifeline available 24/7 for help that is free and confidential.

Dwell

Then Jacob woke from his sleep and said, "Surely God is in this place—and I did not know it!"—Genesis 28:16

Some of the most spiritual people I know are the most present to others. They are not distracted by electronic devices or thinking of what they will say next. Being fully present with someone is sacred. To dwell is to be present, whether it is God's commitment or our own commitment to being present with another. In Genesis, Jacob fell asleep and began to dream of a ladder spanning our earthly dwelling and an otherworldly dwelling where the angels reside. Given Jacob's story of feeling alienated from his family of origin because of his decision to deceive his brother Esau, it is no wonder that he was dreaming of a compassionate and dwelling presence of love. Upon his awakening he exclaims, "Surely God is in this place—and I did not know it!" (Gen. 28:16). God dwells among us, even when we are far from community, far from our spiritual center, or far from home.

Jeff started coming to my church while he was staying at a nearby shelter for unhoused people. He was a brilliant woodworker and worked in construction but ended up on the streets because of his alcohol use. Jeff did not want help from other people. One day, when he didn't show up for something, I went over to his apartment to check on him. When I asked if he was okay, he shouted, "For God's sake, Chad, stop trying to fix me. I can't be fixed."

Jeff was right. I thought I could help fix him, but what he needed was someone to dwell with him in the messy pain of life. He didn't need solutions, programs, books, or me coming to his door to remind him of his responsibility at the church. Jeff needed a friend to be present with him. I often think of him and wonder if he is still alive or if there is a dwelling over his head. But I know one thing: in the two years we knew each other, there was transformation in us both. God was truly in that place with us, dwelling among us as friend and companion, and for those small places of hope, I rejoice.

Reflection Activity: Reflect on what is going on in your life that can't be fixed, but that you simply need someone to witness and dwell with you in the midst of it. Wherever you find yourself, whether in your living room, in a tense meeting, or in the woods, take a moment to pause and savor that space. Become aware of God's presence dwelling within you.

Prayer: When hope seems dim, O God, make me aware of your ever-abiding presence that dwells within me today. Amen.

With hope for today,
Pastor Chad

Tender

And be kind to one another, tenderhearted, forgiving one another, as God in Christ has forgiven you.—Ephesians 4:32

We are in the hands of a tender God. Tender like the first time holding a newborn baby. Tender like holding your mother's hand at a funeral. Tender like sitting at the bedside of a sick loved one in the hospital. God's tender Spirit surrounds all who are heartbroken, embracing us with grace. God is tenderhearted toward each one of us, showering us with affection, compassion, and grace.

A common reason people don't seek support for their mental health is stigma and shame. We think we should be strong enough to get through whatever we are going through all by ourselves. We blame ourselves and shame ourselves, believing if we push through, we can make it, or if we ignore it, it will go away. This is called "self-stigma." It is hard to admit to ourselves when we have reached the end of our capacities. It takes strength and courage to ask for help.

After years of arguing with my husband about the best ways to keep our house clean, we finally decided to ask for help with cleaning. Society's expectations that women should do all the cleaning wasn't working for us. I had to admit to myself and to my husband that I could not keep up with the housework because of my work schedule and its impact on my mental health. Forcing traditional patterns of women doing the cooking and cleaning caused us stress. We gave ourselves permission to do what works best for us, including my husband helping to clean, along with professional help as needed. For the sanity of our marriage, this was a matter of honoring the tender vulnerabilities of admitting our limits and supporting our mental health.

When we are feeling raw, we also might be feeling vulnerable and need a tender place to land. We can trust God's loving Spirit to know just what we need and to meet us exactly where we are: crying in bed with the covers over our head, looking up at the moon for a sign, or balling up our hands in fists. We need a tender God to love us.

Tenderness is not weakness or failure. It takes courage to grow more tender toward ourselves and others. Noticing the tender places in ourselves is sacred. Society teaches us to hide and cover up our vulnerabilities. Yet being tender makes us human. In our tender moments, our hearts are most receptive to love.

Reflection Activity: What does a tender God look like? In what ways do you experience God's tenderness toward you? Take a moment today to be tender toward yourself. You are worthy of tender love.

Prayer: God of hope, I praise you for the tender ways you hold me close to your heart. Amen.

With hope for today,
Pastor Sarah

Taste

O taste and see that God is good.
—Psalms 34:8

Our family went on a trip to Walt Disney World several years ago. We traveled with my parents, and one evening they took the kids so that my spouse and I could go on a date. In our many years of marriage, this may have been one of my all-time favorite dates. We spent the evening at Epcot, traveling around the "world," tasting the different foods from various countries. We had chips, guacamole, and margaritas in Mexico, a beer in Germany, pasta in Italy, and our all-time favorite was the food of Morocco. My taste buds still long to taste those international foods all these years later. There was so much goodness in every bite, and while we didn't eat big meals in each place, having just a taste allowed us to savor each bite and savor our time with one another.

The passage above from Psalm 34 speaks of tasting and seeing that God is good. I imagine this notion of tasting is relevant to any food we enjoy, but tasting is also a spiritual practice and way of being. We can taste the power of friendship or savor a beautiful sunset or a good nap on a lazy afternoon. Sitting on the back porch as it rains can be a taste of the Divine. When we too often taste the bitterness of grief, uncertainty, sadness, anxiety, or depression, then goodness seems far off. Tasting goodness, then, is a radical act of hope. It is a spiritual glimpse of God's all-encompassing presence and love. Each time we savor or taste the goodness right in front of us, we glimpse the grandeur of God.

Reflection Activity: Taste the goodness of your life today, whether in a meal with a friend or spouse, enjoying time in the woods, time in your garden, or an art project, or some activity you enjoy. Take a moment to taste and see the goodness of God. Don't rush. Savor the moment with a posture of gratitude.

Prayer: When hope seems dim, O God, may I taste and recognize your goodness this day. Amen.

With hope for today,
Pastor Chad

Quiet

A time to tear, and a time to sew; a time to keep silence, and a time to speak.
—Ecclesiastes 3:7

I am sensitive to sounds and light, symptoms of my neurodiversity. Too much bright light overhead or too much loud sound triggers my nervous system. The worst-case scenario is my brain gets overstimulated, causing a debilitating migraine headache. My recovery includes becoming still in a room where all light is blacked out, and psychologically I enter into a symbolic womb of God for comfort and self-care. Time and space for silence renews my hope. Silent spaces and time honor the power of silence for the work of inner healing.

Keeping silent creates space for God to show up. In the silence of my mind, I can hear God speaking to my heart. Prayer can be silent meditation. We don't always need words to pray. I know it is ironic for me to say this in a daily devotional about words, but it's true: we can connect to God in the wordless quiet. When we make a spiritual practice to still our minds, we bring awareness to the deeper wisdom of being.

While I was growing up, adults in church told me as a kid to keep silent, like it was a punishment. Being told to be quiet was meant to control us, discipline us, and correct bad behavior. Quietness gets a bad reputation because too often silence is used abusively. In school we were told to "sit still," and it felt like we were being asked to turn off our power or unplug ourselves from the source of our energy. What if we thought about stillness and quiet as invitations to be more in touch with ourselves, rather than to detach ourselves?

What if engaging in silence and stillness is a spiritual practice for liberation? While we are called to advocate for justice, we are also invited to honor silence. I remember when I asked my church leaders if I could take one workday a month for a day of prayer. I was prepared for them to say no because they might not consider prayer as real "work." Thankfully, and to their credit, they enthusiastically said yes. These monthly days of prayer and silence have rooted me in God's love and provided my spirit space to be renewed with hope. Sometimes the right thing to do for mental well-being is to move away from the noise and to decide: "Today I will be silent." God bless the quiet.

Reflection Activity: Find a place today where you can enjoy some quiet time. You are free to choose to be alone or with others. Use this time of quiet to remember you have the power to turn down the noise in your life. And you have the power to break the silence and disrupt the quiet.

Prayer: God of hope, be present to me in the quiet moments of the day. Amen.

With hope for today,
Pastor Sarah

Extravagant

"Other seeds fell on good soil and brought forth grain, some a hundredfold, some sixty, some thirty."
—Matthew 13:8

Extravagance can represent the excessive or over-the-top use of money and resources, such as a private yacht. But presence can be extravagant. Faith can be extravagant. Welcome can be extravagant. Love can be extravagant.

In the passage from Matthew above, the sower is not operating out of a framework of scarcity, worried about how much seed they are wasting. Jesus tells the story of a sower wasting seeds, knowing that some will start to thrive but get choked, and that even others will not yield any growth at all falling on rocky soil. But when seeds fall on good soil, they bring forth a harvest, in some cases a hundredfold. Jesus' story is of a leader willing to be extravagant in their seed tossing, leaving behind any worries over the bottom line, product inventory, or playing the numbers game.

Extravagance is an above-and-beyond kind of love. There may not be a better word for God's love than extravagant, and this brings me hope. God shares such extravagant love with all of us, willing to forgive beyond our worst behaviors. This kind of love is as scandalous as a farmer extravagantly tossing seeds, wherever they may land. An extravagant love thrives and grows where the soil is ready for it, which is why God offers love to us in such abundance. God knows one day we will receive and cherish God's love.

Reflection Activity: What might you do to share your resources in an extravagant way? Give a financial gift to an organization you care about, or volunteer and serve others. Lavish a friend with encouragement. Share yourself extravagantly, not because you are earning other people's love, but because God's love is worth sharing in abundance.

Prayer: When hope seems dim, O God, allow the seeds you have planted in my life to rise into new and extravagant life. Amen.

With hope for today,
Pastor Chad

Adore

While they were there, the time came for Mary to deliver her child. And she gave birth to her firstborn son and wrapped him in bands of cloth, and laid him in a manger, because there was no place for them in the inn.
—Luke 2:6–7

God comes to us in human form and is known to us in the life of Jesus. The birth story of Jesus invites us to adore God in the flesh. On Christmas Eve we sing Christmas carols inviting us to adore the Christ child. I love the candlelight on Christmas Eve as we prepare our hearts to receive this gift of light.

One Christmas Eve, when I was serving in a ministry setting outside of the local church, since I was not the pastor leading worship, I sat in the pews with my family. I noticed my child starting to cry during the Christmas carols. When I asked him what was wrong, he said the music was too loud and the "singing was ugly." We were crowded into the pews, and people sang their favorite Christmas carols with gusto. He was right. It was very loud, and many people were singing off-key.

I took my child out of the sanctuary, and we found a couch in the church library. We snuggled on the couch for a bit. My child began to calm down as I held him close. I began to feel sorry for myself and angry that we were missing the Christmas Eve service. Then I realized: here was the Christ child for me to adore, right in my arms.

Too often, the church casts judgment on families with children who are uncomfortable in traditional settings. This creates a feeling of shame for families and parents who feel guilty. We wonder what we have done wrong. We feel excluded and like we don't belong. What if faith communities could create a culture that honors neurodivergent children and families? What would it look like to adore all God's children, embracing neurodivergent children as the Christ child?

One way my church creates neuroinclusive space in our sanctuary is by including coloring pages for all ages. To support neurodiversity, we have art supplies in the "prayground" space in the front of our sanctuary with fidgets, markers, coloring pages, and soft alternative seating. The children and youth leader on my staff introduced me to a Bible with coloring pages. These ways of engaging our faith invite us to worship and adore the Divine in active and creative ways. We can pray with our hands, with our lips, and with color. We can adore God through the arts, connecting our creativity with the hopeful energy of the Creator.

Reflection Activity: Sometimes we must leave church to feel close to God. What barriers do you experience when you try to worship and adore God?

Take a moment to adore God wherever you are, even if there's no choir of off-key angels singing.

Prayer: God of hope, show me how to better adore the Christ child who appears in unexpected places. Amen.

With hope for today,
Pastor Sarah

Reaching

Then Jesus said to Thomas, "Put your finger here and see my hands. Reach out your hand and put it in my side. Do not doubt but believe."
—John 20:27

Jesus did not shy away from being vulnerable with his close friends. Jesus came to Thomas with his raw wounds, which marked the traumas of the previous week for Jesus and the disciples, Thomas included. If I were in their sandals, I'd much rather forget such an experience and move on with a resurrected Jesus. Yet the resurrected Jesus went straight to the place where the grief and pain of the community were felt most acutely. He asked Thomas to reach out his hand toward those wounds. It is in reaching toward one another that we experience compassion. It is in reaching that we are made whole.

In the first half of 2023, our family faced a significant amount of grief. In that period, four people who were dear to us died, including my grandfather and a saint of God who served as a surrogate grandmother to our kids. On top of these griefs, I was facing significant pressure and stress at work. It was too much to bear. The power of faith communities is that when those who love God love you, they know when to reach out. Close colleagues called, sent text messages, and emailed. Some asked if they could pray with and for me over the phone. We didn't avoid the pain in our lives; instead, we named the hardships and grief together, reaching toward each other with love and compassion.

When we turn toward one another, reaching out whether in grief or joy, challenge or hope, we recognize the resurrected Christ in one another. We are a people of compassion because in Jesus' resurrected state, he didn't call us to a disembodied relationship with him or each other, but rather an embodied sense of real and authentic dealings with what it means to be human. Reach into your vulnerable humanness today.

Reflection Activity: Who might need you to reach out to them with compassion? Call them today. Send them an encouraging text message. Offer to have lunch or coffee or a virtual tea together to share your vulnerabilities. If today is one of those days when the challenges are overflowing and you need comfort or care, who might you call on?

Prayer: When hope seems dim, O God, I reach toward your arms of compassion and ask that you tenderly hold me in all my complex wonderings and wounds. Amen.

With hope for today,
Pastor Chad

Beloved

Beloved, since God loved us so much, we also ought to love one another.
—1 John 4:11

At the heart of the Christian faith is Jesus' teaching to love ourselves and our neighbors. When we experience ourselves as loved, we are considered beloved. In the gospel story about Jesus' baptism, God tells us Jesus is God's beloved. This is a sign to me that God is safe. As a person who experienced emotional abuse as a child from my father, I pay attention to how parents treat their children. I notice things like the words they use when they speak to their children. The Bible says that God calls Jesus "beloved."

People's relationships with their parents are often complicated. One impact of attributing limited human identities and roles to God, such as calling God "Father," is that not everyone has positive associations with their parents. For example, my own father's brain disorder made it difficult for him to express affection and develop healthy bonds with his children. Out of respect for the baggage that many people carry, some people try to use inclusive and non-gendered language when referring to God, even if the Bible refers to God as a Father. Since God is not male or female, we can be intentional about using more expansive language to help more people feel God's love. Using the word "beloved" is one way we can speak of God's relationship to Jesus without using gender. God is the beloved of Jesus. And Jesus is the beloved of God.

Bible passages describing the closeness, affection, and love between Jesus and God give me hope. I am encouraged to know Jesus experienced unconditional love from God, and I desire to experience this unconditional love from God. For people who did not experience unconditional love as children from a parent, receiving this kind of affirmation through faith is a form of redemption and healing from the traumas of the past.

As a child, I enjoyed a close relationship with my maternal grandparents. One of my favorite memories is going to a Saturday matinee with my siblings, cousins, and grandpa. He bought us bags of all-you-can-eat popcorn and all-you-can-drink soda before heading into the cool, dark movie theater. This family outing made me feel special and loved. Now, when I am having a rough mental health day and need a reminder that I am a beloved child of God, I take myself to the movie theater. Grandpa is no longer with us on this earth, but I buy popcorn and soda in his honor. I know he is smiling and enjoying the show from his "balcony seat" in heaven.

Reflection Activity: Today, claim your identity as beloved of God. Imagine God calling you by name, saying, "You are my beloved, with you I am well pleased." Embrace your belovedness today and be free.

Prayer: God of hope, bless me today as your beloved child. Amen.

With hope for today,
Pastor Sarah

Companion

"Do not press me to leave you, to turn back from following you! Where you go, I will go; where you lodge, I will lodge; your people shall be my people, and your God my God."—Ruth 1:16

There is a moment in the final film of *The Lord of the Rings* series, *Return of the King*, where it seems Frodo is no longer able to continue his journey to destroy the ring of power. He is beyond exhaustion and cannot take another step. He and his companion, Samwise Gamgee, have traveled from their home in the lowly shire to Mordor to destroy the allure of evil found in the ring of power. The weight of the ring and the pressure to deliver on its destruction were becoming too much to bear. Then Sam reminds Frodo that none of us face what we do alone.

Sam says to Frodo, "I can't carry it for you. But I can carry you!"[9] Sam is the consummate companion: loyal, brave, a good listener, and fully present to his friend. We all need such people. We all face hardship, uncertainty, pain, grief, and eventually death. There will be moments when what we must carry is too much to bear, and we will need another to help carry us. Our mental health depends on it.

The story of Ruth and Naomi always captures my attention because of their unwavering devotion to each other. They are two women whose lives represent what it means to be fully present to another. Like the support Sam and Frodo give each other, Ruth and Naomi's unwavering commitment to "go where you go" is a model for supporting our mental health with companions who can accompany us during our most vulnerable moments.

[9] *The Lord of the Rings: The Return of the King,* directed by Peter Jackson (New Line Cinema, 2003).

Reflection Activity: As you journey through your day, who are your Ruth and Naomi or your Sam Wise Gamgee? How will you be present with and support each other today? Make a point of thanking them for accompanying you on your journey.

Prayer: When hope seems dim, O God, I know that you have given me companions, soul kin, who remind me I am never alone. Thank you! Amen.

With hope for today,
Pastor Chad

Community

How very good and pleasant it is when kindred live together in unity!
—Psalms 133:1

I used to think the word "community" meant lots of people. Yet the Bible reminds us that community is where two or three are gathered (Mt. 8:20). There is power in community, in remembering that we are not alone. U.S. Surgeon General Vivek Murthy said in 2023 that we are facing a "loneliness epidemic" and that loneliness is one of the leading causes of negative mental health.[10]

A poem I wrote in high school started with this line: "I am alone, thinking of reasons why I don't have a friend to ward off the loneliness." My longtime boyfriend had just broken up with me after a rollercoaster of breakups and reunions, and my best friend had ditched me, all at the same time. As a teenager, I felt totally alone, and it was crushing my mental health. Even though I was surrounded by other people at school and at home, I still felt alone. What I was missing was community, connections, and relationships that sustained my spirit.

Mental health expert Dr. Lisa Miller says in her book *The Awakened Brain* that we are wired for spiritual connection and community.[11] One of my favorite quotes is by United Church of Christ minister Rev. Mike Denton, who praised the power of church potlucks to cure our loneliness. Mental illness is long known as the "no-casserole illness." We take casseroles to people recovering from surgery, but not to people stuck in bed with depression. Perhaps we should create food ministries for people with chronic mental health challenges. Community is therapeutic. We all need reminders that we are not alone.

---

[10] "Our Epidemic of Loneliness and Isolation: The U.S. Surgeon General's Advisory on the Healing Effects of Social Connection and Community," U.S. Department of Health and Human Services, 2023, https://www.hhs.gov/sites/default/files/surgeon-general-social-connection-advisory.pdf.

[11] Lisa Miller, *The Awakened Brain: The New Science of Spirituality and Our Quest for an Inspired Life* (Random House, 2021).

To support my mental health, I schedule monthly brunch meetups with a good clergy friend. She and I both have histories of recovery from mental health conditions and benefit from talk therapy. These are the "casseroles" we give to one another, creating connection over a common experience. We provide an authentic community that is mutually beneficial: compassionate and caring hearts to hold one another's concerns with love. Her friendship fills me with hope and helps to lighten the burdens of ministry I carry, knowing I am not alone.

Reflection Activity: What would it be like to share a casserole with someone who is lonely? Is there someone you might reach out to and offer to bring a casserole or share a meal with? Take time to connect and break bread with someone today. May the Spirit of Christ's love be present to you in the gift of community.

Prayer: God of hope, thank you for opportunities to be in community. Keep my heart open to others. Amen.

With hope for today,
Pastor Sarah

Grief

"Blessed are those who mourn, for they will be comforted."
—Matthew 5:4

Dear reader, let your heart grieve. We spend significant time avoiding what we have lost. We stifle the grief within us to avoid feeling the pain. If Anderson Cooper's podcast *All There Is* teaches us anything, it is that the story of loss in each person yearns for us to lean into our grief. It is, in fact, part of what makes us human. This does not mean we go seeking out grief or pain. It means we do not run away when it arrives at the front door of our heart.

Andrea Gibson wrote the poem "Good Grief," inviting us to "let your heart break, so your spirit doesn't."[12] Grieving is the corollary to loving so deeply that it has the potential to break your spirit. We tend to such love and grief together, letting go to open ourselves to loving anew.

One of the most compelling parts of the life of Jesus is that he did not ignore his own grief. Vulnerably, he wept when he heard of his friend Lazarus' death. He grieved the betrayal of his disciples and his own impending death in the Garden of Gethsemane. There is assurance in knowing Jesus said that those who mourn will be comforted, because the very Jesus who grieved in his own life and has named us as "blessed"

[12] Andrea Gibson, *You Better Be Lightning* (Minneapolis: Button Publishing, 2021), 78.

is also the one who comforts and accompanies us through the valleys of our own grief.

Is there a long-held grief resurfacing in your life, causing depression, heartache, and sadness? Or a recent loss that is raw and fresh? Let your heart grieve knowing you do not face it alone. God weeps with you.

Reflection Activity: Spend time reflecting on Andrea Gibson's sentiment from her poem about grief and let the words wash over you with healing.

Prayer: When hope seems dim, O God, help me to embrace your loving arms in the midst of my grief. Amen.

With hope for today,
Pastor Chad

Compassion

"Sing for joy, O heavens, and exult, O earth;
break forth, O mountains, into singing! For God has comforted the people
and will have compassion on the suffering ones."
—Isaiah 49:13

Did you sleep well last night? Do you have a sleep routine that helps you get a good night's rest? The more we learn about the brain, the more we learn how important consistently good sleep is for our mental health. For me, lack of sleep can lead to a migraine. The only way I recover from a severe migraine is by sleeping for a couple of hours in pitch-dark. Migraines are a sign to take better care of myself. My body is telling me that I am weary, carrying heavy burdens, and need rest.

Serving as the first woman called to be the senior pastor of a church founded in 1857 can be a heavy burden. Breaking through that stained-glass ceiling can make a woman weary. That's why I said yes when I was invited to participate in the inaugural cohort of women pastors from around the country for a graduate certificate education program in executive leadership. The concept was to support and equip women's leadership in the church using best practices from the business world. One of our keynote presenters from a world-class business school shared about their breakthrough research: being compassionate makes you a better leader. Many of us pastors began to wonder why we traveled across the country to hear something we already knew: caring for people and showing compassion counts as good leadership.

Yet even in the church, the model for leadership is dominated by traditionally masculine characteristics and behavioral norms from secular society. As I considered the leadership research coming out of the business school, I let the information sink in. My compassion makes me a better leader. Compassion is not a liability. Compassion opens the pathway to connection, trust, and transformation. Yet for many, compassion is viewed as weakness.

As a compassionate leader, I seek to partner with others to share hope, healing, and joy. Partnerships benefit my sense of well-being. I am a healthier person when I work with a team and can lean on others instead of pressuring myself to do everything alone. It takes self-compassion to acknowledge our interdependency, letting go of society's expectations of success based on individualism, and instead opening ourselves to being blessed with the gifts of leadership others bring.

When it comes time for me to retire from professional life and I no longer supervise a team, I hope I leave a legacy of compassion. There are gifts and skills I don't have for leadership, such as making and managing spreadsheets. There are times when I realize I need help to fulfill a task. I'm learning how to ask for help (and trust me, it's a skill to ask for help, especially for high achievers like me). Asking for help is when I get to apply my leadership style of compassion inwardly and receive for myself the grace I am careful to show to others.

Reflection Activity: Think of a time when you received compassion from others. What need did you have that others met with compassion? Who do you know who is compassionate? Reach out to the person who comes to mind and send them a text message, email, or card in the mail to thank them. If they are no longer alive, then say a prayer of gratitude for the spiritual gift of compassion.

Prayer: God of hope, help me to show compassion to myself when I need to take a mental health day. Amen.

With hope for today,
Pastor Sarah

Presence

They said to each another, "Were not our hearts burning within us while Jesus was talking to us on the road, while he was opening the scriptures to us?"
—Luke 24:32

Have you ever felt overwhelmed so strongly that it nearly takes your breath away? Before one of my most difficult funerals as a pastor, I felt acutely overwhelmed, and it was hard to breathe. My anxiety, grief, and deep worry felt like a debilitating wave crashing onto me. Before the funeral started, I went into the bathroom to pause and to pray because I was afraid the emotion would overwhelm me during the service. So much grief, uncertainty, and swelling of emotion surrounded the circumstances, and I prayed for God to strengthen me to offer all that was needed to comfort the family.

Just as I was about to begin the service, a Carrie Newcomer song came rushing into my mind: "You can do this hard thing. It's not easy, I know, but I believe that it is so. You can do this hard thing."[13] My heart rate steadied, and I began to feel calm, letting go of my worry of controlling my emotions. With God's help, I stepped up to the lectern and led the service with resilience. It was a true gift, and as hard as it was in the moment, I reflect back knowing it was God's presence that not only helped me through the service but also comforted all who were mourning. It was God who "talked with me on the road."

As those on the road to Emmaus discovered in their grief, God is often present when we least expect it. Our hope as spiritual beings is our becoming aware and awake to God's presence while we are "on the road" and to reflect back at moments and celebrate God being there when we were unable to perceive it. How has God been present "on the road" of your journey?

Reflection Activity: Be intentional in recognizing God's presence throughout your day today. When you notice God in your midst, proclaim, "Is not my heart burning within me?"

Prayer: When hope seems dim, O God, keep me present to this moment so I don't miss your close presence near me. Amen.

With hope for today,
Pastor Chad

Care

"Take my yoke upon you, and learn from me; for I am gentle and humble in heart, and you will find rest for your souls."
—Matthew 11:29

If we look closely at the life of Jesus as described in the gospels, we will notice Jesus' self-care routine. Jesus spent time alone, he nurtured his inner introvert, he enjoyed meals with friends, he went to church, he set boundaries by saying no, and he asked for help.

The gospel of Matthew reminds us that following Jesus means experiencing the gentleness and humility of Christ. To be a Christian is to find rest for our souls. Following Jesus is not about proving ourselves

[13] Carrie Newcomer, "You Can Do This Hard Thing," track 9 on *The Beautiful Not Yet* (Available Light Records, 2016).

worthy of God's love. To be a Christian means we rest in God's love. We don't have to do anything to earn God's love.

Our spiritual health is connected to both our mental health and physical health. Yet in society, how we care for our mental health is treated differently than how we care for our physical health. These differences show up in health care coverage, access to quality care, and how we talk about our mental health.

We commonly accept the need to care for our teeth, with many health insurance plans covering dental cleanings every six months. But what about our brain hygiene? What if we could prioritize preventive care for our brains like we do for our teeth? What if we could prevent "brain cavities" such as episodes of depression and anxiety? What if everyone had regular check-ins with a mental health therapist at least every six months? Our mental health requires care because we are human and not robots. How do you care for your mental health?

I'll never forget hearing a pastor talk about when she had to resign her ministry position at the church because of burnout. She said she spent all her time and energy taking care of everyone else until she had nothing left for herself. She realized that she was not being a good steward of her own well-being. Then she asked us, "How are you being a good steward of your own well-being?" This one question changed my life. I went home from that conference and began to imagine what my life would be like if I prioritized being a good steward of myself.

The first thing I realized I needed to do was to get a physical examination. I hadn't had one since I was a kid. Caring about my well-being was not something I knew how to do. But getting a physical was a start. My mental health condition led me to often neglect taking care of my physical health, and since I didn't have any major health concerns, I had been able to avoid doctors. But what if being a good steward of my well-being includes preventive physical and mental health care? This approach to care, focusing on proactive stewardship of my well-being, changed my life and put me on a path to dramatically improve my mental health.

Reflection Activity: God calls us to be good stewards of creation. Churches run stewardship campaigns. But what about your role as a steward of your own well-being? How is that going for you? What's one thing you can do today to show care for your mental health? Do it.

Prayer: God of hope, thank you for your care for every single creature, even me. Amen.

With hope for today,
Pastor Sarah

Love

And now faith, hope, and love abide, these three; and the greatest of these is love.—1 Corinthians 13:13

When I was a young child, I traveled to my great-grandmother's home in southern Kentucky during the summers. Even though it was hot, my great-grandma was always tending her garden and cooking in the kitchen for us. She prepared her food with such love. In the early mornings, she would begin making bacon, eggs, potatoes, and biscuits. The wonderful smell would waft up to our rooms, beckoning us to come down. I often headed downstairs as I heard her banging the pots in the kitchen. I offered my young chef hands to help, and her kindness in allowing me to help was a symbol of her deep love for me.

My great-grandmother's food was her love language and a way for her to show hospitality. Cooking was not the only way she expressed her love. One day, she sat me down on her lap on her bluegrass front porch and said, "Chad, did you know that God loves you? You are loved by God, and I love you." Her words still echo within me all these years later. Every time I get down on myself, experience debilitating anxiety, or find myself in a space of sorrow, I recall my great-grandmother's words to me in her loving southern accent, and I am transported into the loving arms of God.

Reflection Activity: Who has made you feel loved in this world? Bring their names and faces and words to your mind, and remember you are loved. Savor them and the ways they have demonstrated for you what love feels and sounds like. Who will you remind today that they are loved?

Prayer: When hope seems dim, O God, let love be my source of strength. Amen.

With hope for today,
Pastor Chad

Hold

For I, the Holy One, hold your right hand; it is I who say to you, "Do not fear, I will help you."—Isaiah 41:13

God is our helper in times of trouble. The Bible is filled with stories about people crying out to God for help. Why is it so hard to ask for help in our lives today? It's one thing to get help for yourself as an individual. It's another thing to ask for help as a couple, whether married or partnered. It feels foolish to be in a partnership and to admit that you need help making the relationship work. How do you know when to ask for help or when to give up and leave? How do you know when it is time to hold on to someone close and when to let them go?

One of the most tender and taboo topics I've ever written about is when an intimate relationship, like a marriage, is impacted by mental health experiences. As my spouse and I are nearing our twentieth wedding anniversary, we navigate mental health in our marriage daily. This has been true since our first date. For some marriages, holding on to each other through mental health experiences is the pathway forward. For other marriages, letting go is the best path forward. Often, it's hard to know whether to have and to hold or to let go.

My mother once told me she didn't believe in divorce, but she needed to end her marriage because it was no longer safe to stay. She let go of marriage so she could hold on to abundant life. It's complicated. What does it mean to hold on to a marriage that brings more stress than joy, more despair than hope, more pain than pleasure?

We navigate these questions in our marriage with the support of therapists, one for each of us and one for our marriage. We depend on three professionals to help the two of us. We are lucky to have good health insurance that covers an unlimited number of therapy sessions. On the days when we wonder if we should let go, we bring this question into therapy.

No one told us when we got married that mental health experiences would carve themselves into us, cutting deep. We were unprepared to face the reality of what the combination of our family histories of mental health would do to our relationship. The one thing that has helped the most is the permission to hold on if we want to, but also to let go if we need to. We choose to hold on one day at a time.

My husband gives me a bouquet of fresh flowers each week. Sometimes it's the weekly special from the florist, sometimes it's a dozen red roses. The flowers represent his ongoing care and love for me. It's a thoughtful gesture that never gets old. The flowers brighten my mood and lift my spirits. Even though navigating mental health realities in our marriage is difficult, my husband still gives me flowers. I hold on to the goodness of this gift, and that counts for something.

Reflection Activity: What has surprised you about mental health and its impact on your relationships? Have any of your relationships ended because of the impact of mental health? Invite God's Spirit to reveal to you which relationships to hold on to and which relationships you might need to let go in this season.

Prayer: God of hope, reveal to me what I need to hold on to in this season. Thank you. Amen.

With hope for today,
Pastor Sarah

Sanctuary

You are a hiding place for me; you preserve me from trouble; you surround me with glad cries of deliverance.
—Psalms 32:7

Sanctuaries are often thought of as sacred physical spaces of refuge from the storms of life. There is a holiness to their beauty that transcends time and space. Yet sanctuaries can also be more than a building with beautiful stained glass. I also think of sanctuary as the way we offer refuge to one another or, as a line in a song sings, "Lord, prepare me to be a sanctuary."[14] Our lives can be the sanctuary by which the presence of God offers safety and wholeness.

Indiana folk singer and poet Carrie Newcomer's song "Sanctuary" gets to the heart of why this notion of refuge is so important to spiritual life. She sings: "Will you be my refuge, my haven in the storm? Will you keep the embers warm when my fire's all but gone? Will you remember and bring me sprigs of rosemary, and be my sanctuary 'til I can carry on?"[15]

There are days when it is hard to carry on. Because of the stigma of mental health experiences in our culture, we need spaces of refuge where our experiences of depression, ADHD, bipolar disorder, or social anxiety are not judged as weakness. Sanctuaries are spaces where we can draw strength and hope in our stories. Newcomer's words contain the heart of sanctuary in the spiritual life, where we offer to one another to be a refuge in the storms that surround our lives. Whoever is a sanctuary for you today, I invite you to take refuge there as your "hiding place," surrounding you in "glad cries of deliverance." Trust that you are loved beyond measure.

Reflection Activity: Who will keep the embers warm in your journey when your fire is nearly burned out? How do they offer you sanctuary? Draw near to them, and find respite there.

Prayer: When hope seems dim, O God, may I find a sanctuary of hope in my day. Amen.

With hope for today,
Pastor Chad

---

[14] Randy Scruggs and John Thompson, "Sanctuary" (Whole Armor Music and Full Armor Music, 1982).

[15] Carrie Newcomer, "Sanctuary," track 6 on *The Beautiful Not Yet*, (Available Light Records, 2016).

Release

"I will give you the keys of the kindom of heaven, and whatever you bind on earth will be bound in heaven, and whatever you loose on earth will be loosed in heaven."—Matthew 16:19

I grew up in the Midwest, where along the highway there are billboards advertising Jesus. One billboard alongside a soybean field says, "Jesus, take the wheel." For about a year in college I was part of a Christian fellowship that emphasized personal salvation based on a relationship with Jesus Christ as Lord. After confessing sin and belief in Jesus Christ, we were offered the chance to be born again and to be cleansed of our sinful nature.

I have since released these beliefs. They do not serve me well. A few months after my conversion experience, I began to feel uncomfortable. There was strong emphasis in the organization on judging whether someone was saved. In fact, saving lost college students seemed to be the primary goal of the fellowship organization.

Leaving this campus ministry was hard because of the loss of community, but it led to a time of rich spiritual growth. I was free to find other people to help me live out my Christian values. I joined a student volunteer organization and began spending time in the downtown shelter for the unhoused. There I met Christ among the unhoused people staying overnight at the shelter, and I discovered the joy of my salvation in community with the people God loves.

One harmful teaching of that college Christian fellowship related to policing our romantic relationships. The group leaders used the Bible to argue that women needed to remain virgins until marriage and that marriage was only between a man and a woman. These rules were confusing, and what was often a time of freedom and expression related to sexuality during college years became a time of control and policing. It has taken me decades of work in therapy to begin healing from the harm of those teachings. To release the negativity around my body, I spend time at the gym because engaging my body in empowering ways and feeling good in my body is healing. Exercise helps me release negativity and spread positivity throughout my body, from my mental health to my physical health. This is an ongoing part of my life's work to embody hope.

Reflection Activity: Is there something, someone, an organization, or a commitment you are holding onto that no longer is a good fit for you? What might it be like to release that which no longer serves you? Today, ask God to help you release whatever is holding you back from spiritual growth.

Prayer: God of hope, reveal to me what I need to release in this season. Thank you. Amen.

With hope for today,
Pastor Sarah

Loving-Kindness

Your steadfast love, Holy One, extends to the heavens, your faithfulness to the clouds.—Psalms 36:5

Our first family pet was a beagle foxhound mix named Abby. She was a sweet and caring companion. She loved our family and friends with a fierce kind of love. Abby was known for jumping up on anyone who would come into our home. It was her special way of greeting others. It could be a bit much for those who aren't used to an excited dog greeting them at the door. We were concerned about how she might respond when we brought home our first child. The evening we brought our daughter home, instead of jumping and wagging and being her normally excited self, Abby came up to us in a calm and curious manner. We slowly put down the car seat in the entryway, and Abby slowly extended her nose toward our newborn, welcoming her with a deep and abiding love.

When Abby died eight years later, my wife, our daughter, and I went to the vet with her. The vet gave us a private room to say our goodbyes, and we sang these words to her as a form of a loving-kindness prayer: "May she be strong and healthy, peaceful, and at ease; may she be filled with loving-kindness and be happy." And we let her go.

Abby's loving-kindness still surrounds me, and the moment of our family grieving together and extending to her in return the words of a loving-kindness prayer will live in my memory for a very long time. This is how loving-kindness works in the world. We extend love to one another just as God extends it all the way to the clouds. In a world that stigmatizes those who struggle with mental health, may we find ways to receive and extend loving-kindness to the world.

Reflection Activity: Go outside on a loving-kindness adventure. When you encounter a human, an animal, or a business, extend to them the whisper of the loving-kindness prayer. Such energy will radiate towards them in love. Choose to whisper loving-kindness to others in your life as you move towards a family member, a friend, an enemy, trusting that their mental health and spiritual well-being are held in the arms of God as you pray. If you are not able to go outside, consider sending loving-kindness to people you know in email, text, or other messages.

Prayer: When hope seems dim, O God, you remind me that your love has no end. May it be more than enough for all that I need to live faithfully into this day you have made. Amen.

With hope for today,
Pastor Chad

Value

"Look at the birds of the air: they neither sow nor reap nor gather into barns, and yet your heavenly Parent feeds them. Are you not of more value than they?"—Matthew 6:26

I've learned to find value in stability. Growing up in a home that lacked stability because of my father's untreated bipolar disorder, I learned that constant change and uncertainty were just part of life. I became skilled at navigating chaos. We moved across the country when I was entering fourth grade; my dad kidnapped my brothers when I was in middle school; my cousin was arrested for murder then sentenced to death when I was in high school. All five of us kids held multiple jobs to help my mom pay the bills and keep us fed. We worked as babysitters, waiters, newspaper carriers, and the Easter Bunny.

Today, I value keeping a schedule, being rooted in one place, and planning ahead. Still, I appreciate the value of doing what it takes to survive. We deepen our interdependence as we deepen our rootedness. We do the best we can with what we have until a better way unfolds. Many people are working hard just to get through the day. What if we dared to hope for more than only survival?

Mental health flourishes when we can move our energy and focus beyond survival mode, navigating constant chaos. My freshman year in college, I made the personal decision to be a vegetarian because I wanted to honor the interconnectedness of all of life and do my part to decrease suffering in the world. I wanted to live out my values through my lifestyle choices. Being kind to the planet is connected to being kind to my bodymind, and my mental health benefits from being a vegetarian.

God values mental health. What would it look like for communities, schools, and faith communities to value mental health? To value something is to be transparent about it. Notice how much our culture focuses on beauty, youth, and being rich. What if we focused more on mental health and placed value on connecting people to mental health resources?

Reflection Activity: What values dominated your childhood? How have your values changed over your lifetime? What would it be like for you to value your own mental well-being today? Do one thing today to honor the value of your mental wellness.

Prayer: God of hope, help me value and prioritize practices that improve my mental health. Amen.

With hope for today,
Pastor Sarah

Play

"Then I was beside God, like a master worker; and I was daily God's delight, rejoicing before God always, rejoicing in God's inhabited world and delighting in the human race."—Proverbs 8:30–31

I stood at the entrance of the historic labyrinth inside of Grace Cathedral in San Francisco, preparing to step into the path leading toward the sacred center and back out again. The great labyrinth teacher Lauren Artress told our class the key to walking a labyrinth was allowing whatever we encountered on the path to be our teacher. It might be a thought, an emotion, an object in the path, a sound, or a smell. Whatever we encounter has the potential to teach us something about our spiritual journey.

I stood at the entrance with Lauren's wisdom ringing in my ears, ready to accept what God might be saying. Then it happened. My perfect contemplative, calming, peaceful, and insightful prayer walk through the labyrinth was ruined. Grace Cathedral is open to the public most of the day, and just as I made my way around the first bend in the path, a little girl and her mother came walking into the sanctuary near the labyrinth. The mother began looking at all the beauty around her, staring at the huge Gothic ceilings. While the mother was lost in awe, her daughter began skipping and singing. In fact, she skipped with joy right through the labyrinth and in front of my walking path. She didn't start at the beginning, using the entrance to make her way through the labyrinth. No, like a car cutting you off in traffic, she went right through the middle, skipping past me on her way to another side in the sanctuary without a care in the world.

I was furious. How could this mother let her daughter just skip through a sacred labyrinth like that? Doesn't she know there are rules for the labyrinth? How rude. How insensitive. The little girl ruined my focus. I kept walking, feeling frustration and disappointment. Then I remembered Lauren's instruction. As I finally reached the center of the Labyrinth, I spent some time breathing, sitting, and reflecting. I realized this little girl was not being thoughtless or rude, and she hadn't ruined my sacred walk.

The interruption was my teacher. The little girl reminded me to have joy, to be playful, and not to take things so seriously. The proverb speaks of Lady Wisdom as being playful before God, and the labyrinth walk invites us into a playful life. With so much heaviness weighing on us daily, Lady Wisdom invites us into a playful life, too.

Reflection Activity: Find a way to play today. Put aside your work or productivity, and play a card game, read a book, play a sport, dance, listen to an album from start to finish, or watch a movie. Each of these has the capacity to heal and bring joy during mental health experiences or challenging days.

Prayer: When hope seems dim, O God of laughter and playfulness, guide us and allow us to delight in all that you have made so that we may be filled with your joy. Amen.

With hope for today,
Pastor Chad

Savor

"No one has greater love than this, to lay down one's life for one's friends."
—John 15:13

I wonder what it was like for Jesus to savor the moments he spent with those he loved. In scripture, we catch glimpses of times Jesus is with his disciples sharing a meal in the upper room, at a dinner party, or around a campfire. Then there are moments when Jesus is alone and in prayer, savoring his time with God.

My mental health experiences with depression led me to greater awareness of moments worth savoring. I wonder about Jesus' personal encounters with mental health experiences of anxiety, stress, and depression, times when he felt the weight of the world on his shoulders. His humanity shines through in scripture with stories about his anger, despair, heartache, and frustration. I'm grateful Jesus is fully human in his full range of emotional and mental health, evident in the stories about him in the Bible—stories when Jesus felt intense emotions such as when he wept overlooking the city of Jerusalem.

Jesus' life also created moments for others to savor, such as his mother, Mary, as she held her newborn baby in her arms. The friendship between Jesus and Mary Magdalene gave them heart connections Mary Magdalene savored her whole life. Jesus helps me savor my own life, knowing there is grace for me as a child of God. One way my family savors life together is through listening to live jazz music. My son, Carter, plays jazz on his tenor saxophone and performed at the world-famous Jazz Kitchen in Indianapolis as part of a youth jazz program with Butler University. I savor these moments to honor the gifts of God coming to life inside of him.

Reflection Activity: How have your personal mental health experiences shaped moments in your life that you savor? Recall an experience or relationship that you savor. Make time to express gratitude to God for this gift in your life.

Prayer: God of hope, thank you for the delights of this life. Help me savor every good thing. Amen.

With hope for today,
Pastor Sarah

Friendship

"I do not call you servants any longer, because the servant does not know what the master is doing. But I have called you friends."
—John 15:15

At a retreat center surrounded by beautiful woods and a lovely flowing river, a group of colleagues and I took a walk, despite a drizzle of rain. The path before us was fine and easy until it wasn't. When we turned a corner onto a downhill section of the trail, the terrain became slippery. At the first turn, one of my colleagues seemed hesitant, anxious even, about whether to continue. Seeing our friend uncertain of whether they could make the journey, we offered our arms so they would be stable in getting down to the next level. There were several moments on the journey down to the river when we really needed each other to stay upright and safe. We offered one another the support of our arms as we continued down the path.

Our friendship required a sense of deep awareness of when the other needed support. Friendship is a commitment to another, not because we can get something from the other, as though the only reason for friendship is transactional in nature. Friendship is a mutual giving of the self for the thriving of a friend, as well as our own flourishing. In the spiritual context, friendship is an essential part of how we journey with God. A friend is support, accountability, trust, compassion, and insight when we realize we cannot traverse our journey alone.

In John 15, Jesus offers his hand in friendship. He takes away the notion of a servant, which would make the relationship transactional. Rather, Jesus embraces the give and take of love. That is risky. He risks being hurt or betrayed. In fact, that is exactly what happens with his disciples. Yet the unwavering love of God is such that even in spite of these things, God still thinks of us as friend, companion, one for whom they would reach out an arm to ensure that we get down the hill as it rains and mud threatens to sweep us toward harm. Our mental well-being and personal flourishing require us to ask for an arm of support when we need it. Our mental health depends on the power of such friendship.

Reflection Activity: Which friends support your mental health and spiritual journey? What is support like in your relationship? Take a moment to offer that support to a friend today, or if you need support, reach out and ask to be accompanied.

Prayer: When hope seems dim, O God, remind me that you offer the gift of friendship and that a community of care surrounds me. Amen.

With hope for today,
Pastor Chad

Cherish

When the cares of my heart are many, your consolations cheer my soul.
—Psalms 94:19

When I was a child, I had to fit all my cherished belongings into a Strawberry Shortcake pillowcase. We were fleeing domestic violence in our home and had to escape in the middle of the night. We moved from California to Missouri to live with my grandparents. I don't remember what I put into my pillowcase, but I do remember the thing I most cherished I had to leave behind: my best friends.

I still think about my early childhood friendships and cherish the memories of our time together. Katie and Katherine were my two best friends, and I had to leave them without saying goodbye. This traumatic experience left me heartbroken, anxious, and depressed.

It was the mid-1980s before email, cell phones, text messages, and social media. I wrote them both letters with pencil and paper (plus cute puffy unicorn stickers) that I put into the mail the first year after I moved away from California. Over time, those letters decreased until we stopped writing, as we began to make other friends. I've stayed in touch with Katie through social media, but Katherine I lost touch with completely. Despite the loss, I cherish these memories of my early childhood friendships because they remind me of the deep well of joy inside of me.

One way I cherish my friendships today is through prayer. My friends comment on the text messages they get from me asking how I can pray for them. They tell me how meaningful it is to be thought of and prayed for regularly. Prayer is a form of love. When I pray for my friends, I connect with them through the Spirit of love, and this connection makes me feel loved, too.

Reflection Activity: Think of a relationship in your life that you cherish. What about the relationship or memory brings you the most joy? If possible, reconnect with that person and let them know you cherish them, or offer a word of gratitude to God for the blessings of this person in your life.

Prayer: God of hope, I know you cherish me as your child. I receive the gift of being loved. Amen.

With hope for today,
Pastor Sarah

Fruit

"Every tree that does not bear good fruit will be cut down and thrown into the fire. Thus you will know them by their fruits."
—Matthew 7:19–20

Right off the edge of our back porch is a peculiar plant—peculiar because it is one of those bushes that produces food for the wildness of creation all year round. It adjusts its food and fruit with the seasons. In the fall, it blossoms into a beautiful pink flower where the bees and hummingbirds can receive nourishment. In the summer, it produces small white flowers. In the spring and winter, the bush produces little berries, and the birds come and feed. This is a full bush, and its growth can often seem like a nuisance because it will get in the way of the path off our porch. It grows so much that it often needs trimming. As challenging as this intrusive bush can be, we thoroughly enjoy watching its fruit and flowering offering sustenance to our birds, bees, and other animal neighbors.

We often know whether something brings life to us by what fruit a person, circumstance, or idea produces. One of my key litmus tests for knowing fruits is to ask the question: "Does it bring life?" Jesus' use of fruit trees to illustrate what brings life can extend to nearly all areas of the spiritual life, from spiritual practices to mental health supports to the experience of a worshiping community. Jesus tells us to examine and taste the goodness of the fruit produced right in front of us. If it bears good fruit, it is worth celebrating and gravitating toward with frequency. If it does not bear good fruit, it might be okay to let that thing go for now.

Reflection Activity: As you journey through your day, is the form of prayer you engage in something that brings life? Are the friendships you maintain bearing a fruit that allows you to grow and transform as a human person? Are the mental health supports you have in place sustaining you through the ups and downs? Whatever you face today, ask the question: "Does it bring life?"

Prayer: When hope seems dim, O fruit of the vine, let your sweetness remind me that I shall know peace and hope everlasting. Amen.

With hope for today,
Pastor Chad

Remember

For whatever was written in former days was written for our instruction, so that by steadfastness and by the encouragement of the scriptures we might have hope.
—Romans 15:4

Taking time to remember what made it possible for me to survive the traumatic experiences of my life is one of the most powerful experiences in my ongoing recovery from complex post-traumatic stress disorder (CPTSD). As a person of faith, I try to remember the "God moments" even during the most difficult times. I ask the question: "Where was God when this happened?" It's a difficult question for me because the first story I tell myself is that the trauma happened because God abandoned me. We not only need second chances, we also need second stories—the story behind the story. The second story is the "God story" behind the "OMG" story.

When I think about my past traumas, I ask for God to reveal to me where hope was present. Then I try to remember the hope and the helper. For me to still be here, alive today, something and someone kept me going. What was it? Who was it? I remember my high school teacher, Mr. George Frissell, stopping me in the stairwell one day at school to ask me what was wrong. This simple yet powerful gesture of care and kindness lifted me out of the shadows. My teacher took time to notice me.

Trauma can erase good memories, obscuring the hopeful parts of our stories in the shadows. It's good to remember how far we have come and the traumas we have overcome by the grace of God. It's good to remember the "second story" of where God is revealed. I enjoy research and writing projects that help me remember the God stories that have been forgotten. The process of writing an essay, poem, memoir, or other writing project allows me the luxury of a deep dive into topics of special interest. Writing is healing for me and invites me to remember God's faithfulness, even in times of difficulty.

Reflection Activity: What do you remember about how hope came into your life during difficult times? Understanding our traumatic memories by remembering what or who helped us survive can bring healing and peace. Take a moment to express gratitude to God for not abandoning you and to remember how much God loves you.

Prayer: God of hope, reveal to me the power of remembering as a path to healing. Amen.

With hope for today,
Pastor Sarah

Grounded

But their delight is in the law of God, and on his law they meditate day and night. They are like trees planted by streams of water, which yield their fruit in its season, and their leaves do not wither. In all that they do, they prosper.
—Psalms 1:2–3

One day, during a season of spiraling hopelessness, depression, and uncertainty, my wife said to me, "Let's go for a drive. I know a place we can go to get away and reflect." I had no idea where we were going, but we got in the car and she drove us to the Irvington neighborhood on the east side of Indianapolis. In the middle of this dense urban neighborhood was a four-hundred-year-old oak tree called "The Great Kile Oak." A small group in the neighborhood had created a little pocket garden and sacred space with a picket fence, a description of the history of the tree, and some picnic tables where one can sit and reflect. This oak is an oasis in the middle of the tense world of the urban setting that surrounds it. The tree is eighty-seven feet tall, and its arms stretch out as if to welcome you with a hug as you walk toward it from the street. I certainly needed a hug at that time. The only word I could say as I stepped out of the car was "wow"!

We sat for a long time on the picnic tables, just staring up at the tree's grandeur. Then I decided to step toward the oak and get up close to the trunk. I placed my hand on its rough exterior, surrendering my burdens and worries upon its grand foundation. I asked the oak: *What do I do?* I heard these words: "Stay grounded." It was not the full answer to the challenges I was facing at the time, but this simple advice served as a reminder that spiritual grounding keeps us centered in the strength of God.

We all experience highs and lows, especially when there is stress or emotional distress. We all have moments in our lives when we are uncertain of what to do or where to go next, and our mental health and spiritual center long for such grounding. No matter what burdens you carry or what keeps you up at night, faith offers us a circle of protection in ways that remind us we are not alone—and like a mighty oak hugging us with tenderness, God's enduring love always encircles us.

Reflection Activity: Find a sacred place where you can reset in the midst of the chaos and hectic pace of the world. Allow such a space to ground you as you engage in spiritual practices that make sense to you and your mental health. Step away from the grind, and pause within your grounding space. Allow it to uphold you in strength as you re-enter your daily world.

Prayer: When hope seems dim, O God, help me to stay grounded today so I can face all that will come my way. Amen.

With hope for today,
Pastor Chad

Transform

Do not be conformed to this world, but be transformed by the renewing of your minds, so that you may discern what is the will of God— what is good and acceptable and perfect.
—Romans 12:2

Stories have the power to transform our lives. To tell the true story is to heal. To transform is to change, to evolve, and to be rebirthed. We don't transform by ourselves but in community. Feeling isolated and alone is common during mental health experiences of depression. It's hard to "ask for help" when we barely have energy to get out of bed.

One of the most transformative moments in my mental health experience was when I realized I carried self-stigma about my own need for help. When I let go of the shame of needing help, I began to feel better. Just knowing I could ask for help when I needed help felt like a weight lifted. I now have professional support as well as friends who I can reach out to when I need help to navigate a mental health-related experience that feels overwhelming. By transforming shame and stigma about asking for help, the culture of silence and shame begins to change.

We know that exercise is good for our bodyminds. How often do we consider the benefits of meditation, prayer, music, medication, therapy, and connecting to loved ones? Don't give up on yourself. Transformation is slow work, but the benefits last a lifetime. Imagine yourself transformed.

Reflection Activity: Do you carry any self-stigma, shame, or guilt about needing help? How easily can you ask for help when you need it? Who do you trust when you need support?

Prayer: God of hope, transform my self-doubt into faith and my self-stigma into self-love. Amen.

With hope for today,
Pastor Sarah

Worth

See, I have inscribed you on the palms of my hands; your walls are continually before me.—Isaiah 49:16

While I was cleaning out one of our cluttered closets, a box filled with several photos of our family over the years came tumbling out onto the floor. Sorting through these photos, bringing back memories, I uncovered one photo that left me breathless. There she was: my great-grandmother Cecil. I was the first of her great-grandchildren, so we had a special bond. She was sitting on her front porch, swinging with me as an infant sitting on her lap. Though I have no memory of that moment, it immediately reminded me of one of the most profound moments of my spiritual life. Sitting on her lap at that very spot years later, she would tell me of my infinite worth in the eyes of God. I took this newly found photo and placed it right next to my bed, so whether I am rising or resting, I am reminded that I am worthy, that I am deeply loved, beyond compare and without condition. And, dear reader, so are you.

God has "inscribed you on the palms of my hands." When the world tells us we are not worthy or we find ourselves in a dark hole of depression, it is easy to forget these words or the places where we know this spiritual reality for ourselves. I hope, dear reader, you have someone in your life who helps you see your infinite worth. If not yet, I want you to borrow my great-grandma Cecil's words of love.

Reflection Activity: Perhaps you have that one memory or photo or place in creation that can remind you of your infinite worth in the eyes of God. Find a way to connect with that place and those words today.

Prayer: When hope seems dim, O God, sit me down on your lap and remind me that I am inscribed on the palms of your hands. Amen.

With hope for today,
Pastor Chad

Rebirth

Praised be the Abba God of our Savior Jesus Christ, who with great mercy gave us new birth: a birth into hope, which draws its life from the resurrection of Jesus Christ from the dead.—1 Peter 1:3 (The Inclusive Bible)

As someone who frequently feels inadequate and unworthy of love, each day is an opportunity for rebirth. In my quiet time of spiritual reflection in the morning, I am reborn by the power of God's unconditional love. If I am open to receiving God's grace, then God's Spirit invites the new day to be one of spiritual rebirth. But God doesn't force spiritual rebirth onto us.

Some days I believe I am strong enough to get through the day without God's help. How foolish! Those are the days I most need God's help. But my pride keeps me thinking I don't need God. This is why daily spiritual practices keep me grounded in God. Thank God for the daily invitation to be in relationship with the Spirit, trusting in God.

My dependence on God's grace humbles me and reminds me of the relationship God desires to have with us. Throughout the Bible, we read stories about God's desire to be in relationship with us: from creating the first humans in the garden in Genesis; to the sign of the covenant rainbow in the sky; to the birth of Jesus, who is Emmanuel, God with us, to the Risen Christ, whose Spirit remains with us always. The sacred stories remind us that our beginning and ending are with God. Each day we are born again in the Spirit of God's love. The Bible is a book about rebirth. It's never too late to be born again. No emotion lasts forever. New life comes.

Water is a powerful symbol of life, in the sacrament of baptism and in water's presence on the planet and in our human bodyminds. Whenever we use water for bathing or drinking, we are invited to consider opportunities for rebirth; energetically we are cleansed, and physically water helps purify our bodyminds. Taking care of our physical needs, such as drinking plenty of water each day, benefits our mental health and improves overall well-being.

Reflection Activity: What does it mean for you to experience rebirth in your daily life? If God's Spirit could provide you with all you need for today, what would you ask for? Take a moment now to ask God to bless you with rebirth. May God give you every good thing for your soul.

Prayer: God of hope, I am ready for rebirth. Amen.

With hope for today,
Pastor Sarah

Gifts

Now there are varieties of gifts, but the same Spirit; and there are varieties of services, but the same God; and there are varieties of activities, but it is the same God who activates all of them in everyone.—1 Corinthians 12:4–6

Each of us is born with gifts to share with the world. Some are musicians or painters; others are writers and poets, coaches or mentors, athletes, gardeners, and people who can mediate conflict. I am a poet, musician, spiritual director, stained glass artist, avid pickleballer, and writer. I love learning the saxophone, and while I will never be John Coltrane, I love what music brings to the world. I love making a good piece of stained glass to give away to others. This long, slow art is well worth every minute when I recognize the look on a person's face when they observe their glass piece for the first time. I love writing and reading poetry. I may not be among the giants in poetry, but I have come to understand that, yes, my voice as a poet does matter.

I was in a conversation with a friend about writing poetry, and I found myself sharing with them in a self-deprecating way, "Well, I love writing poetry, but I am by no means Mary Oliver." They stopped me right there and set me straight, responding, "Chad, the world does not need you to be Mary Oliver. The world needs you. The world needs your voice, your poetry." They celebrated my gifts and empowered me to see the uniqueness of my contributions to the hope and joy of the world. You, too, have gifts to offer this weary world. Those gifts matter. They bring hope and are needed so others may recognize the flourishing of their own gifts. So write the book. Paint the canvas. Run the race. Plant the garden. Build the deck. Sing the song. Lead the team. Bake the cake. Mentor the youth. Teach the students, and join the band. You and your gifts are so desperately needed in this world, and one does not need to be in some sort of professional status to give them.

Reflection Activity: Choose one of your gifts and share it today, not for the sake of gaining affirmation but simply because your gift matters and brings you joy. Daydream beauty and wonder, or write in your journal, because it gives you life and strengthens your mental health.

Prayer: When hope seems dim, O God, let me invest in my own gifts today and celebrate them with joy. Amen.

With hope for today,
Pastor Chad

Awaken

There is one bodymind and one Spirit, just as you were called to the one hope of your calling.—Ephesians 4:4

Numbing is a way to survive times of intense emotional pain in our lives. During difficult seasons of life, I have numbed myself by working too much or drinking a glass or two of wine. In January of 2020, I decided to give up alcohol when I realized my urge to drink came from my desire to decrease uncomfortable emotions like sadness, anxiety, stress, and insecurity. Now when I have these emotions, I know how to pay attention to the feelings. Instead of numbing out, I tune in. Feelings are my bodymind's way of telling me something about myself.

An important part of my mental health recovery is to move from numbing myself to being awake to my emotional self. When I awaken to my emotions, I am in touch with my full identity as a child of God. I am not my flaws and insecurities and the worst things I have done or left undone. At my core, I am made in God's image. At my core I am good because God made me good. Instead of identifying myself by the bad things that have happened to me, I can remind myself that my value goes deeper. Hope comes from awakening to the image of God within.

It's so easy to go numb in a world that hurts too much. Sometimes that's the way we survive. But what if there is another way to live? With the help of friends, mentors, and therapists, I am supported in my efforts to stay awake to my core self. The transition from numbing to awakening is life-changing and critical to the process of recovery. The path of sobriety blesses my mental health, and it's a path more people are exploring. Self-acceptance and self-love come when we no longer feel the need to mask our emotions with alcohol. Awakening to myself, I honor who I am becoming. I celebrate the community of sojourners who also seek to awaken to the complexity of emotions and discover ways to be present to them instead of numbing out. Knowing that I am not the only one who turned to alcohol to stop feeling pain reminds me of my deep humanity and connects me to the human experience of suffering.

Reflection Activity: Do you have experience with numbing yourself to help survive something painful? What would happen if you could awaken to your true value as a child of God? Ask God to awaken within you the ability to transform numbing behaviors into recovery practices leading to more abundant life.

Prayer: God of hope, awaken my sleeping heart so that I may fully receive your love. Amen.

With hope for today,
Pastor Sarah

Mountain

I lift my eyes to the mountains—where does my help come from?
—Psalms 121:1 (NIV)

Have you ever had the perfect song come along at just the right time in life? There are songs whose words and images offer a profound connection with your soul, challenging you to ask deeper questions, opening you to mystery, and encouraging you.

I had one of the most difficult years of my life in 2024. Dislocating and breaking my ankle, I could not put weight on my right leg for six weeks and endured two surgeries. I made the best of it, but as a physically active person, I found myself wrestling with loneliness and the complete sense of dependence upon my family to help me do everything. During this time, I fell into depression, grasping every day for any shred of hope. Just before my second surgery, Coldplay released their *Moon Music* album. Over the difficult months of recovery from surgery, this album became a balm to my soul. In this album, I discovered the song "IAAM," which stands for "I am a mountain." My year of hardship was often met with prayers like that from Psalm 121: "I lift my eyes to the mountains—from where does my help come?"

The power of "IAAM" is that it uses the imagery of a mountain to remind us of the strength God provides to overcome adversity and hardship. The song proclaims: "I got this feeling, and now nothing is frightening. I got this feeling I can summon up lightning. I got this feeling, and just what it is, God only knows."[16] The song continues in offering resiliency and strength: "Stood on a sea of pain, let it rain, let it rain, let it rain. I'll be back on my feet again, because I am a mountain." Heading into 2025, I made this song my anthem for the year, and it carried me through the highs and the lows.

Mountains are central to the vital stories of faith in nearly every religion. On top of mountains, spiritual insights or experiences of God's presence occur. Mountains can also, like trees, address our being grounded when we surrender ourselves to God. Living in the Midwest, mountains are not part of my daily landscape, yet they can be a profound image of strength in difficult times. How does the majestic structure of mountains provide you with peace when your mental health seems uncertain?

Reflection Activity: Where does your help come from in difficult times? Reflect on an idea of a mountain or picture, or if you live among the mountains, allow them to be a source of hope today.

Prayer: When hope seems dim, O God, may I trust in your mountain majesty. Amen.

With hope for today,
Pastor Chad

Alert

Let your steadfast love, O Holy One, be upon us, even as we hope in you.
—Psalms 33:22

I have hypervigilance, which means I am alert to sounds, movement, and changes in my environment. This developed out of the sense of danger I

[16] Coldplay, "IAAM," by Coldplay, Holter, and Max Martin, track 7 on *Moon Music* (Parlophone / Atlantic, 2024).

felt growing up in a chaotic household. Many people stay alert for safety reasons, and it's how we learned to navigate the world to stay safe and alive.

Being alert to the movement of the Spirit in our midst is a spiritual practice I am cultivating with intention. Working with a spiritual director, together we ask the question of where God's Spirit is moving. To be alert to the Spirit takes intentional focus and time to reflect. To be alert to the Spirit calls for stillness and silence. To be alert also calls for movement and experiencing new environments.

Traveling to new places and exploring new sights and sounds uses my gift of alertness in rewarding ways. I experience mental health benefits from traveling because of the opportunity to "get out of my head" and be in the present moment, absorbing all the new sensory inputs. Travel also helps me get out of the rut of ordinary day-to-day demands of life. There is also the relief and joy that come from returning home after a time away. When I travel, I often feel closer to God because I am paying more attention to the movement of the Spirit.

The same abilities to be alert to keep safe can also support spiritual growth. Perhaps that is why some of the most spiritually mature people I know have endured significant trauma. We have learned how to pay close attention to often unseen movements all around us and within us. When we pay attention to the Spirit, we notice the steadfast love of God. We can place our hope in God's steadfastness.

Reflection Activity: Be alert to the movement of the Spirit today, making time for stillness and silence. See what you notice arise from within you. Ask God to reveal a sign of God's presence with you today.

Prayer: God of hope, help me stay alert to your surprising grace today. Amen.

With hope for today,
Pastor Sarah

Awe

Let all the earth fear the Holy One; let all the inhabitants of the world stand in awe of God.—Psalms 33:8

We all need to experience awe rising within us. For some of us that might be an emotionally moving piece of music or an inspiring physical space of beauty. It may be a holy conversation with a trusted soul friend. Awe is the opening between wonder, hope, and inspiration that often leaves us speechless.

A few years ago, an art museum in Indianapolis created a digital art exhibit. I stumbled across it one afternoon as I walked through the main floor of the museum. As I walked in, meditative music enveloped the space with a calming effect. I immediately felt at ease. Visuals automatically drew my attention toward the ceiling. Digital images of trees waved back and forth in the wind, ocean-like waters moved in and out of the shore, and galaxy-like images took the onlooker into a different dimension altogether. The pavilion has low seats that allow you to lie back and look up from the ground floor. It didn't take long to experience a euphoric sense of awe and wonder as the music and images transported me into a holy presence.

Over the years since I discovered this sacred space, I have found myself going there during a lunch break and simply resetting or grounding myself. Other times I go there when I'm facing difficult decisions or not knowing quite what to do with a situation. I sit and look up and pray, asking God to guide me. I took my staff to the museum for lunch to spend time sitting together in the space and praying for one another, those we serve, and the wider world. Though this art space reflects the awe found in physical creation, its sheer beauty beckons us to join the psalmist in proclaiming, "Let all the inhabitants of the world stand in awe" (Ps. 33:8).

Reflection Activity: How do you seek to capture a sense of awe? Find your space of awe, and let it ground you for the living of these days.

Prayer: When hope seems dim, O God, draw me toward spaces and moments of awe that renew. Amen.

With hope for today,
Pastor Chad

Altar

And Saul built an altar to the Holy One; it was the first altar that he built to God.—1 Samuel 14:35

"Make an altar by your bed." This was the advice of my yoga teacher, Lori. I had met with her the week prior to my radical hysterectomy, seeking help as I navigated my fears and uncertainties about the surgery and the recovery. Building an altar by my bed was something I had never done before. I had never considered the possibility of creating a personal altar at home as an expression of faith. I thought altars were only for churches. It turns out, people have been creating home altars for centuries.

During my medical leave, as I rested in my bed, I found the bedside altar to be a powerful reminder of God's healing presence in my body. I felt God's encouragement to take my time healing. I felt the Spirit's comfort as I navigated discomfort and fatigue. The altar was a visible sign of the power of faith. The altar also reminded me that I am not alone. I have my spiritual angels looking over me, as well as my in-flesh angels, friends and family helping me heal. My mother came to stay with me for several days and made her famous curry egg salad sandwiches, the same recipe she used when she visited me over a dozen years ago during my maternity leave. I've learned to call upon all the angels living on this earth and in heaven above to help because there is no award for the person who suffers the most.

Even though the surgery was several years ago, I still have my bedside altar, with a few changes. I've added a singing bowl and a crystal. I have my icons of Jesus, Mary, and Mary Magdalene. I have my purple cross I got in New Orleans, covered with pearls and festive beads. I am encouraged by these beautiful symbols of God's unconditional love. This sacred altar eases and blesses my mind. It's like a big inhale and exhale for my brain.

Reflection Activity: Do you have an altar in your home? If not, consider making a simple altar. It could be at your bedside, in your kitchen, or by a window. Make a space to remind you of the presence of God's loving care for you, a clear sign of the Spirit dwelling around you and within you.

Prayer: God of hope, make an altar within my heart. Amen.

With hope for today,
Pastor Sarah

Mending

When Jesus saw him lying there and knew that he had been there a long time, he said to him, "Do you want to be made well?"—John 5:6

Mending requires tending. To mend that which is broken or cracked requires going directly to the source of the pain and not avoiding or running from it. I uncovered this reality a few years ago while creating a piece of stained glass art. As I was getting to the end, I turned over the piece only to discover that one of the outside pieces had cracked. I couldn't believe it, and while it wouldn't have been a big deal earlier in the project, that it was soldered together and framed made it much harder to mend. I asked my stained glass teacher to help me fix the crack. We unframed the broken side and discovered that in order to make the entire piece whole again, we had to tend exclusively to the one piece that was broken. We heated up the soldering iron and slowly reheated the solder lines until they melted and freed up the glass to be pulled out altogether.

This is spiritual work. Long, slow, intentional tending to the pieces of us that need mending. I could have left the crack in the stained glass piece and given it away as intended, but it would always have the broken piece present. To fix it, I had to go directly to that which was broken and slowly, methodically, and even prayerfully tend to the ways the crack was held together with the other pieces. Once I was able to free the broken glass from the rest of the piece, I was free to bring in the new. That which is broken can mend, but such mending requires tending directly to the cracks and pressured harm that created it in the first place.

When there is emotional or spiritual pain in life, sometimes it is easier simply to run away or ignore it because of the discomfort. The only way toward healing is not around or over the pain, but through it and in it. Jesus asks a question: "Do you want to be made well?" Each of us has different paths toward healing because our cracks and pain take on different shapes. But together and in the healing strength of God's presence, we can turn toward our pain with tenderness and trust we are surrounded in the deepest of care.

Reflection Activity: How are you becoming aware of the cracks or breaks within your spiritual and mental health journeys? Welcome the mending, and do so with abundant care and grace for yourself.

Prayer: When hope seems dim, O God, mend my heart when it is broken. Amen.

With hope for today,
Pastor Chad

Freedom

Now the Holy One is the Spirit, and where the Spirit of God is, there is freedom.—2 Corinthians 3:17

I experienced a feeling of freedom when I learned about neurodiversity, the affirmation of brain differences as naturally occurring diversity, as seen in biodiversity. Neurodiversity is an identity we can choose for ourselves that celebrates our brains as not broken, abnormal, or diseased, but as good and whole. My complex post-traumatic stress disorder (CPTSD) and the migraines I experience are a type of brain disorder, but these realities don't completely define who I am. We are not our diagnoses. We are children of God.

Identifying as neurodivergent means I can celebrate the way I think, feel, and experience the world because of how my brain works. Freedom comes from not feeling a need to pretend these differences do not impact every aspect of my life, from work to school to family and friends. There is freedom in taking off the mask we often hide behind to fit into society's expectations.

One place I enjoy celebrating my neurodiversity is at a sporting event for the WNBA basketball team, the Indiana Fever. I let my neurodiversity shine as I jump up and down for points scored and scream for joy at the perfect pass. During one game, the woman next to me asked if I was related to any of the players on the court. I said, "No, why?" And she answered, "You cheer like you're their mom!" I took that as a great compliment. My enthusiasm for the game is hard to hide, and why should I? I embrace the freedom to enjoy myself.

Freedom to be our true selves opens the door to experiencing the deepest forms of divine love. I thought I could hide my neurodiversity from everyone, including myself and God! Yet this impulse to hide also creates barriers in relationships. Without the mask, we can more authentically connect with our truest selves and embrace the good news that God loves us just as we are—fully neurodivergent and fully good.

Reflection Activity: Neurodiversity may be a new concept to you, or you may already think of yourself as neurodivergent. Imagine the freedom we can experience or offer others by honoring their full, unmasked identities. Think of a way today that you might affirm yourself or someone in your life who reflects God's gift of neurodiversity. May God's love be known in this affirmation.

Prayer: God of hope, thank you for the neurodiversity of all of creation. Amen.

With hope for today,
Pastor Sarah

Waiting

Wait for God; be strong, and let your heart take courage;
wait for the Holy One!—Psalms 27:14

I grew up in rural Illinois as the grandson of a farming family. My parents were educators, so we did not run the family farm, but it certainly played an important role in the rhythm of our life. Waiting is not the greatest gift of an industrialized and marketing-heavy society. Those who live close to the land teach us something different about waiting, and this has been a sacred learning for me.

For a long time, I couldn't understand why my family would always talk about the weather. Weather is often cast as the topic of conversation for when we are trying to avoid the real topics. In our family, the weather is not small talk; it is made of the spiritual art of waiting. When my grandparents and uncles speak of the weather, they are speaking of the crops that have yet to come, the most essential part of their livelihood.

They spend their days tending to the most essential parts of the fields and animals so that their flourishing can occur.

The weather demands we wait. In times of drought, we wait for rain to fall. Other times the rain is so abundant that it is hard to maneuver a tractor in the field and the seeds run the risk of too much water for growth. The time between planting seeds until an entire field is harvested is a season of waiting, trusting, and allowing forces outside of our control to bring abundance. Waiting is spiritual work because it requires trust in that which we cannot yet see. Sometimes our mental health experiences of waiting too long cause anxious thoughts of the unknown to grip us with unrelenting fears. Yet with the strength of the Spirit and the support of community and mental health accommodations, waiting can be a holy work of letting go so that we can trust God with our lives.

Reflection Activity: What is it that you are needing to let go of so that you can trust God? What seeds has God planted in your life that need the space and time of watering, sun, and the abiding care of God's Spirit before they are harvested?

Prayer: When hope seems dim, O God, help me to wait for you with courage and surrender in anticipation of new life to come with the harvest. Amen.

With hope for today,
Pastor Chad

Change

The Holy One bless you and keep you; the Holy One make their face to shine upon you, and be gracious to you; the Holy One lift up their countenance upon you, and give you peace.—Numbers 6:24–26

Change can be stressful. In times of stress, anxiety, and overwhelm in my family, we often turn to the wisdom of the Serenity Prayer by Reinhold Niebuhr: "God grant me the serenity to accept the things I cannot change, courage to change the things I can, and wisdom to know the difference." The key to being at peace and feeling the blessings of God in the midst of change is to know what you have the power to change and what is not in your control to change.

Most of the time, we are powerless to change most of the dynamics impacting our lives. For example, a stressful job must be endured until a new one can be secured because the job pays for food and housing. Yet frequently the most overlooked powerful change is found by searching within our own minds and adjusting our perspectives. In realizing the only person I can control is myself, I harness my energy and turn it inward. I ask myself, *What do I have the power to change?*

I am constantly growing and changing as a lifelong learner. I read books, journals, research, and studies and attend lectures, seminars, conferences, and retreats. I continue taking graduate-level coursework because learning is stimulating and fun. I enjoy being around other students who think differently and offer new perspectives on the world. Free, quality public education has the power to change the world and improve the quality of life for everyone.

Peace of mind is power. Focusing on improving my behavior, attitude, and perspective honors my own agency and power to change what is within my control. I can reflect on my situation, then respond with a changed mindset. God grants us serenity to accept that which we cannot change. Mental clarity and serenity bless us with peace. The peace of God dwelling within our minds is a daily grace we can nurture and cultivate. When I let go of my need to control others or control outcomes, I am investing in my mental well-being.

Reflection Activity: What is one thing about your life you wish were different? How might you move in a positive direction toward that change? Who might you ask to help you as you move toward making a change today?

Prayer: God of hope, help me make one change today for the better. Amen.

With hope for today,
Pastor Sarah

Gratitude

We must always give thanks to God for you, siblings, as is right, because your faith is growing abundantly, and the love of every one of you for one another is increasing.—2 Thessalonians 1:3

Gratitude is a celebration of our interconnected life with all of God's creation. We have all too often oversimplified gratitude by writing down a list of all the things for which we are grateful. Yes, things. While I have found deep value in writing down what I am grateful for as a prayer practice, rarely do I find myself gravitating to celebrating things I possess. Instead, my gratitude gravitates towards the relationships that surround my life: it's about the people.

I began a new spiritual practice of gratitude while I was on a sabbatical. I went to my local craft store to look for some colorful greeting cards. I bought cards with blank insides so I could fill in the entire card with writing from my own pen. Each day of my sabbatical, I prayed over a friend, a relative, or a spiritual soul-kin and wrote them a personal note. Some were spiritual mentors or companions, others were longtime friends, and some were colleagues. I wrote about a time when they had influenced my life, supported me through a hard time, or inspired my faith or mental health journey. Often these letters would come at just the right time in another's life, serving as a deep well of strength when it was needed.

Gratitude for friendships, soul-kin, and our deeply held human relationships remains at the heart of who God has made us to be. The author of Second Thessalonians begins his letter with a typical greeting, followed quickly by a word of gratitude as he expresses just how much he has witnessed their growth in faith. Such intentional words of what we witness in another's life can make all the difference in that person's life. We can boost positive mental health for others when we witness what makes them shine.

Reflection Activity: Take a moment during your day to contact someone for whom you are grateful for because they have shown up in your life with love. Send an email, a text message, or a handwritten note to them. Allow this to be a moment of practicing gratitude as a spiritual exercise.

Prayer: When hope seems dim, O God, remind me of the people you have placed in my life, and may I be filled with gratitude. Amen.

With hope for today,
Pastor Chad

Spirit

And hope does not disappoint us, because God's love has been poured into our hearts through the Holy Spirit that has been given to us.—Romans 5:5

Hope is the work of the Holy Spirit. Hope is a gift. This is why taking time for spiritual practices is connected to cultivating hope. Being more attuned to the Spirit makes the world a more hopeful place. Once we start paying attention to the presence and movement of the Spirit, we begin to embody hope for ourselves and for others.

I am certain the Holy Spirit led me one day to embody life-saving hope. Driving home from work, I turned into our neighborhood off a busy street. As I drove down the street toward a stop sign, I saw a child running down the middle of the street in front of my car. I quickly pulled the car over and got out. I looked for adults around and saw no one. The child was alone. I called her, and immediately I could tell she was confused.

The child was nonresponsive to my calling out to her, ignoring my efforts to get her attention. I realized she was a nonverbal autistic child. I gently placed my arms around her in a circle, not touching her, but guiding her to the side of the road where she would be safe. A minute later I heard a woman halfway down the block yelling for the child. The child had gotten out of the backyard and had run away. Grateful her granddaughter was safe, the woman thanked me for helping her grandchild.

I thank God I was focused on driving, with my eyes on the road, and not distracted looking at my phone. I thank God for the Spirit who heightened my senses that day. I very easily could not have seen the little girl in the road; she was so small. The Spirit must have guided my actions, because I'm not sure how I knew what to do or how she knew she could trust me. Thankfully, the Spirit is wise and compassionate, keeping us safe from harm. I know we were lucky that day. Too often, distracted drivers cause untold devastation and death in collisions with automobiles, bicycles, pedestrians, and motorcyclists. The Spirit can guide us to safe practices while driving, but it's up to each of us to put down our phones and keep our eyes on the road.

Reflection Activity: Think of a time when the Spirit interceded for you during a time of uncertainty or danger. How did you know it was the Spirit guiding you? Make time today to connect to the Spirit and express gratitude for the saving grace of the Spirit's protection from harm.

Prayer: God of hope, pour out your Spirit upon me and guide my path today. Amen.

With hope for today,
Pastor Sarah

Liminal

Now God said to Abram, "Go from your country and your kindred and your father's house to the land that I will show you."
—Genesis 12:1

A classic experience of a road trip with young children is the inevitable question from the back seat, thirty minutes into a multi-hour drive: "Are we there yet?" Because children have a hard time understanding time and space, this is a legitimate question. Where are we on the journey, and how far are we from our destination? These are liminal spaces, the spaces between where we have been and where we are going. Such in-between spaces are incredibly uncomfortable for those who need to be in control or who dislike living with the unknown.

In a world obsessed with controlling the future and with our minds captivated by painful stories from the past, it is understandable why we do not enjoy the discomfort of the liminal. There is comfort in what is known, in trusting what is stable. There is even joy in imagining a future we cannot see because it engenders hope for new life. But remaining in the mystery? Staying in what is unknown and uncertain? No, thank you.

Liminal spaces call us to live in the present moment. Abram's experience in Genesis 12 is a prime example of such a liminal space. Abram was in his elder years, and God called him and Sarai to journey to a new land. God offered promises that seemed improbable or impossible. Surely leaving what is known and safe to journey through doubt, uncertainty, and fear hardly seems wise. The future seeks to allure us with possibility. Liminal spaces, on the other hand, call us to the present moment, to be here and now, and to trust our past and future to a God who will light the way. Instead of avoiding the unknown, uncertainty, and discomfort, we are invited to journey with Abram and Sarai, and the Israelites after them, into something entirely new. In the liminal moments in between, God's hope abides.

Reflection Activity: Find a doorway, and hold yourself there to pause and pray. The threshold of a doorway offers us a liminal space to reflect. Take a few moments in that doorway to reflect on where you have been and where God may be taking you.

Prayer: When hope seems dim, O God, help me to go into the unknown and in the in-between, trusting you with the way. Amen.

With hope for today,
Pastor Chad

Creativity

So if anyone is in Christ, there is a new creation: everything old has passed away; see, everything has become new!
—2 Corinthians 5:17

Play therapy, music therapy, and art therapy are all part of our family's approach to caring for our mental health. Creativity uses parts of our brain that help express our thoughts and emotions. Releasing tension from the bodymind, creativity unblocks energy stuck inside.

In my senior year of high school, I created an art portfolio filled with abstract paintings with bold colors and geometric shapes. Creativity eased my depression and allowed me to express myself through movement of color on the canvas. The creativity of my classmates also inspired me to express myself more freely.

One of my art classmates is now an elementary art teacher. She shares the artwork of her students as a reminder of the creativity inside all of us, whether or not we are "good" at making art. Being good or bad is not the point. The point is to process and release energy, both negative and positive, through creative play and expression.

One of my favorite things to do is visit the local art museum and gardens. I feel alive when I explore the art exhibits and learn about what inspired the artists to express themselves. Surrounding myself with art stimulates the creativity in my brain and awakens my senses to imagine what might be possible. If I am feeling mentally stuck or uninspired, a trip to the art museum is a wonderful way to revitalize my mind and nourish my well-being.

Reflection Activity: One of my favorite ways to pray is through coloring. I recently purchased a Bible for coloring and creative journaling. How do you like to express your creativity? Everyone has a creative spark, even if it's hidden. Ask God to unlock your creativity and guide you to express yourself in a way that is playful and freeing.

Prayer: God of hope, help me to embrace creativity as a spiritual practice. Amen.

With hope for today,
Pastor Sarah

Beauty

How beautiful you are, my love, how very beautiful!
—Song of Solomon 4:1

I love that sacred texts all over the world acknowledge beauty as part of celebrating creation. The Bible speaks of the beauty of trees, rocks, birds, and mountains, to name just a few from physical creation. In the Song of Solomon, one lover acknowledges the absolute beauty of the other. It is, yes, erotic in some way, but it has always felt deeper than that to me, as if acknowledging a sense of raptured awe. Beauty points to a place of awe and amazement as part of the spiritual life, and because God has created everything in God's image, there are infinite possibilities for celebrating beauty all around us.

Spiritual life does not limit beauty to that which we can observe. Beauty can also be something we create. Some create incredible music or poetry, while others build community, design comedy, or embrace painting or pottery or knitting, thus co-creating with God. Beauty has the capacity to sustain our spiritual life, and it can be that which nurtures our mental health in times of joy and struggle.

My wife told me she planted some zinnias in our raised garden beds. I did not know much about the flowers at the time, but I quickly learned from my "mother of butterflies" spouse just how many different species zinnias attract. These amazing plants are stunning in color, ranging from purple to yellow and orange. These bright colors and the flowers' sweet nectar call forth butterflies, bees, hummingbirds, and goldfinches, sometimes all at the same time.

Some days, all it takes to settle my spirit during a time of stress or anxiety is simply to walk over to the windows near our garden and see how the zinnias create a community of beauty among those that come to seek their friendship. We all need a window into such beauty. When you are struggling, overwhelmed, depressed, exhausted, or just plain need a break, what form of beauty do you draw upon?

Reflection Activity: Embrace beauty. Search for it today as you move, work, pray, and surround yourself with community. It is everywhere if you will search for it.

Prayer: When hope seems dim, O God, help me to see the beauty all around me. Amen.

With hope for today,
Pastor Chad

Brave

Be strong, and let your heart take courage, all you who wait for God.
—Psalms 31:24

I've been told I am brave to share, through writing and speaking, my personal stories about mental health experiences. I'm not sure how I feel about being described as brave. For me, sharing these stories is necessary for my own healing. It is part of my advocacy efforts to break the silence and end the stigma and shame of mental health experiences such as depression, anxiety, bipolar disorder, complex post-traumatic stress disorder, addiction, suicidality, and more. Is it brave to seek to make life better?

When we notice a person being brave, chances are they are motivated by a different desire than to be brave. What motivates me is the desire to be free from shame and stigma, as well as to help other people who have experienced the hurt, pain, and complexity of chronic mental health experiences. I want to help prevent suicide. I want to encourage others. It gives me hope to know I can do something to help prevent or lessen the suffering of others.

Is this brave? That's not why I do it. To me, brave is the person navigating a mental health crisis who keeps inhaling and exhaling. It is brave to stay here, especially when everything inside your head tells you it's time to go. The bravest person in the room is the person who wants to escape this life yet makes it to the next breath. To everyone who has been there: you are brave. Thank you for staying here with us.

It is brave to ask for what you need. When I ask for bright overhead fluorescent lights to be adjusted because they are triggering a migraine, this is brave in a world that treats accommodations as a burden. I dream of a world where we won't have to be brave all the time. I dream of a compassionate world that proactively provides accommodation menus as a standard sign of hospitality. I dream of a world where it is no longer considered brave to stay alive.

Reflection Activity: We often don't realize the heavy weight people carry around inside their bodyminds. And we would be surprised to know which of our neighbors, colleagues, friends, or family have thoughts of suicide. Suicide is preventable, and everyone deserves support. Please help share the text or call 988 Lifeline; it's available 24/7 as a free and confidential way to get emotional support.

Prayer: God of hope, thank you for the reminder that it is brave to receive help. Amen.

With hope for today,
Pastor Sarah

Mutuality

Beloved, since God loved us so much, we also ought to love one another. No one has ever seen God; if we love one another, God lives in us, and God's love is perfected in us.—1 John 4:11–12

One of the congregations I served created a "Blessed Are the Caregivers Gala" where members of the church sat with a caregiver's loved one while they attended this celebration that included a meal and a concert. In an often thankless and tireless act of self-giving, these folks cared for a sibling, parent, and even a child. Caregivers were encouraged to invite a friend or loved one to join them so they could enjoy the gift of community during their night out. The beautiful black and gold tables welcomed one hundred people into a night of laughter, tears, gratitude, and joy. While it was only one night and certainly would not alleviate overall exhaustion, we hoped that in building this time together they would know they were not alone and would learn about support resources in the community. It was a beautiful expression of mutuality, the giving and receiving of care. Our lives and stories are intricately intertwined, calling us to such mutuality. In fact, the first letter of John reminds us mutual care is how God is revealed and made known in us.

How is love enacted reciprocally with others in your life? How is your life intertwined with the lives of others? It can be easy to give to others and sometimes harder to ask for help in return when we are overwhelmed, especially when the stigma of our mental health experiences becomes a barrier to our healing. We don't want to seem dependent on others. Mutual love is vulnerable and invites us into a vision of love toward one another.

Reflection Activity: Take a moment today to check in with someone you know is struggling. Ask what they might need. If you are struggling, trust the soul-kin in your life enough with your vulnerability to express that you might need their presence.

Prayer: When hope seems dim, O God, help me to love others as you have so loved me. Amen.

With hope for today,
Pastor Chad

Unique

Know that wisdom is such to your soul; if you find it, you will find a future, and your hope will not be cut off.—Proverbs 24:14

One of my favorite aspects of Christian faith is the good news that each of us is made uniquely in the image of God. There is tremendous pressure in our society to fit in, to be like other people, to think like everyone else, and to act "normal." Yet many of us find being "normal" to be stifling, boring, and dull. We can become depressed when we don't have an outlet to express our own uniqueness.

If we are made in God's image, then our uniqueness is a gift from God. When I get an idea that excites me, sometimes I am afraid to share it with others because I am worried about what they will think. Is it strange? Is it stupid? Is it silly? Are my ideas good enough? These fears crush the gift of being unique. Being unique can feel lonely.

The Enneagram is a personality tool used to give framework to various human personality types. I am an Enneagram Three, which means I am driven by achieving goals, being successful, and performing. These attributes have blessed me in many ways, but the shadow side is that I ignore my own feelings of inadequacy and unworthiness, often feeling the need to earn love and approval. What makes me unique is how I choose to use my personality and characteristics to shape my life and how deeply I am willing to explore the root causes of my insecurities. When I am most secure in who I am, that is when I can most feel free to be my unique self.

I dream of a world where we are safe to express all our unique ideas, expressions, thoughts, feelings, and desires in ways that are healthy and that honor of the Spirit of God flowing through us. A world where everyone is free to be themselves will help alleviate loneliness and isolation and help us express the unique gifts we add to the world.

Reflection Activity: Remember a time when you felt like you were in a unique situation or had a unique idea. Were you able to share with anyone about it? Sometimes we hesitate to share our unique experiences for fear of rejection and judgment. We worry something might be "wrong" with us. Take time to reflect about the ways God has given you a unique life.

Prayer: God of hope, help me to honor my own uniqueness today. Amen.

With hope for today,
Pastor Sarah

Surprise

I am about to do a new thing; now it springs forth, do you not perceive it? I will make a way in the wilderness and rivers in the desert.
—Isaiah 43:19

God says through the prophet Isaiah, "I am about to do a new thing ... do you not perceive it?" There are days when it is hard to see what forms of the sacred are seeking our attention. In fact, just as it is surprising that rivers will be made in a desert, some experiences of the sacred come as a surprise. I might refer to these moments as "sacred surprises." And they seek our attention every single day.

At the birth of our second child, my spouse was having a difficult time getting through the first half of our birth experience. It had lasted a good portion of the day, and the nursing staff was about to turn over for the night when Parker walked into the room. Parker was a male labor and delivery nurse who looked exactly like Jerry Garcia. I am not kidding. The look on my wife's face told me she was uncomfortable with a male nurse in this very vulnerable moment, yet my guess is Parker had seen that look before. Our doula decided to ask a question: "What made you want to be a labor and delivery nurse?" He stroked his gray beard and replied, "I guess I just like to see new life come into the world." Her question was as much for my wife as it was for her. Sly doula. Brilliant, but sly.

After several more hours, in some of my wife's most difficult moments, Parker was there supporting her, encouraging her, and asking what she needed with a tenderness that caught me by surprise. In fact, his compassion, advocacy, and attention to detail caught us all by surprise. When they wheeled my wife into the OR for a C-section, he noticed she was having cramps in her legs. Parker stayed with us through the operation and advocated for her to the surgeons because she was in pain. He could have gone on to other patients, but he stuck with us until the end. When our child finally made her appearance, it was Parker who walked this bundle of love to me and, handing her to me, said, "Daddy, there is someone here waiting to meet you."

On the surface, we would have never perceived this moment with Parker as sacred, yet it was a river in the desert, a way in the wilderness. Sometimes the things we need most that embody the holy are right in front of us. They come to us as sacred surprises. They come looking like Jerry Garcia in scrubs to bring new life into the world. God is doing a new thing in your life today. Do you not perceive it?

Reflection Activity: Do something new today, something you normally would not do, even if it is uncomfortable. Open yourself to a new friendship, perhaps with an unlikely person. Allow this moment to break you open to perceive God's presence and surprise you with joy. Or perhaps do something surprising for another person and listen to their reaction of gratitude.

Prayer: When hope seems dim, O God, let your sacred surprise bring something new into my life. Amen.

With hope for today,
Pastor Chad

Hope

For surely I know the plans I have for you, says the Holy One, plans for your welfare and not for harm, to give you a future with hope.
—Jeremiah 29:11

A hospice chaplain told Sarah, "We are so good at having funerals for hope." He's right. We are good at burying hope because we have lots of experience of losing hope. Hope dies in the headlines of the 24/7 news cycle. There's a tipping point to media consumption where overexposure erodes our mental health. Hope gets lost in the shadows of the world's despair. For many of us, hope is buried ten thousand miles below sea level.

Both of us used to be more intentional about fasting from social media, but lately we find ourselves addicted to the mindless scrolling and constant news of global crises. After an hour goes by, we catch ourselves wondering, *What world do I live in?* What is worse, we feel helpless to stop the world from falling apart. The future seems bleak. The future appears to be without hope. Reality can easily escape us as we immerse ourselves online, with artificial intelligence and algorithms designed to manipulate our insecurities, what computer scientists call "brain hacking."

We worry about the future as parents and as citizens. What kind of world will our children inherit when we are gone? The level of harm being done to the planet is irreparable. The welfare of children living in poverty around the world is heartbreaking. Yet into these realities, the biblical prophet Jeremiah reminds us that God desires for all of creation to have a future filled with hope. Our work as people of faith is to figure out what we have the power to change to make this hopeful future possible.

It's easy to get overwhelmed and shut down because the needs of the world are so great, too much for one person to handle. Let's start small. Today we can be mindful about our engagement with technology and social media. We can create moments of hope throughout our day when we set aside our phones, laptops, and other devices. We can take a moment to center ourselves, take deep breaths, and meditate on God's unconditional love for us. Reminding our nervous system that we can rest in the love of God invites us to an inward peace at the soul level. Our faith can help improve our mental health through the practice of meditation on God's love.

Our futures are filled with hopeful moments when we make time not only for authentic connection with God, but also for authentic human connection. This devotional book was born out of such moments. As writers and friends, we decided to meet monthly over a meal without phones and laptops and obligations and just find a place to dream about what other kinds of stories God is emerging among us apart from the 24/7 news cycle.

Surely there is a different way, we wondered together over our savory chai lattes. The kind of hope we all long for can be born when we let go of distractions and embrace community. We can invite others to join us in technology-free sabbaths. We can resurrect hope in our daily efforts to show kindness to one another. Hope isn't a feeling we sit around and wait for; it's a practice we cultivate together. We invite you to join us in answering the call of the Spirit, fulfilling the longing for deeper connections. Together, let's resurrect hope.

Reflection Activity: Make time today to put away your phone and devices for thirty minutes. Go outside. Spend time in nature or imagining yourself in a beautiful environment. Invite someone to join you if possible. Notice signs of hope in the natural world around you. Where do you experience glimmers of hope in creation?

Prayer: God of hope, when I feel lost and alone, comfort me with a new spirit of life. Amen.

With hope for today,
Pastor Sarah and Pastor Chad

Acknowledgements

Thank you to the United Church of Christ Mental Health Network, the United Church of Christ Disabilities Ministries, and the national setting of the United Church of Christ for partnering with me in the work of mental health and disability justice. Thank you to First Congregational United Church of Christ of Indianapolis, who called me in 2018 to serve as their first woman senior pastor. Thank you to my therapist, spiritual director, clergy coach, mentors, Community of Practice, and friends for all the support and prayers. Thank you, Chad and Chalice Press, for dreaming this dream into being along with me. Thank you to my family for accepting and loving me just as I am. Thank you to God for blessing me with a hopeful heart and mind.

—SGL

Thank you to the Indiana-Kentucky Conference of the United Church of Christ and its Mental Health Network for allowing my work in spiritual formation and mental health to intersect. I am grateful for my spiritual director, Judy Fackenthal, who helps me stay grounded and supported in the midst of my ministry. Thank you to my Conference Minister colleagues, UCC National Ministries partners, countless spiritual friends, and all the mentors who have guided me and walked alongside my journey. I am grateful, Sarah, that we saw the same vision for this intersection of spirituality and mental health and that you were willing to take the risk with me to share our stories with the world. Thank you to my family, Shannon, Isa, and Lukki, for your love and compassion. Thank you to the Spirit, who nudges, prompts, calls, forgives, and loves me in all things and through whom my hope abides.

—CA

Mental Health Resources

- Anxiety and Depression Association of America, www.adaa.org
- American Foundation for Suicide Prevention, www.afsp.org
- Interfaith Network on Mental Illness, www.inmi.us
- Mental Health America, www.mentalhealthamerica.net
- Mental Health First Aid, www.mentalhealthfirstaid.org
- National Alliance on Mental Illness, www.nami.org
- National Lifeline, call/text 988
- National Institute on Mental Health, www.nimh.nih.gov
- Trevor Project for LGBTQ Support, www.thetrevorproject.org
- United Church of Christ Mental Health Network, www.mhn-ucc.org

Youth Mental Health Resources

- American Academy of Child and Adolescent Psychiatry, www.aacap.org
- Child Mind Institute, www.childmind.org

Dementia Resources

- Alzheimer's Association, www.alz.org
- For people caring for someone with dementia, www.alzheimers.gov
- National Family Caregivers Association, www.caregiveraction.org